Parens

Raising
them Up

ISRAEL WAYNE

First printing: April 2020

New Leaf Press, P.O. Box 726, Green Forest, AR 72638
New Leaf Press is a division of the New Leaf Publishing Group, Inc.

ISBN: 978-0-89221-765-6
Digital ISBN: 978-1-61458-749-1
Library of Congress Number: 2020934456

Cover by Diana Bogardus

Unless otherwise noted, Scripture quotations are from the English Standard Version of the Bible, copyright © 2001 by Crossway, a publishing ministry of Good News Publishers. Used by permission. All rights reserved.

Scripture quotations noted NKJV are from the New King James Version, copyright © 1982 by Thomas Nelson, Inc. Used by permission. All rights reserved.

Scripture quotations noted NIV are from the New International Version®, copyright © 1973, 1978, 1984, 2011 by Biblica, Inc.™ Used by permission of Zondervan. All rights reserved worldwide.

Scripture quotations noted NLT are from the New Living Translation, copyright ©1996, 2004, 2007, 2013, 2015 by Tyndale House Foundation. Used by permission of Tyndale House Publishers, Inc., Carol Stream, Illinois 60188. All rights reserved.

Scripture quotations noted NASB are from the New American Standard Bible®, copyright © 1960, 1962, 1963, 1968, 1971, 1972, 1973, 1975, 1977, 1995 by The Lockman Foundation. Used by permission.

Scripture quotations noted KJV are from the King James Version of the Bible.

Please consider requesting that a copy of this volume
be purchased by your local library system.

Printed in the United States of America

Please visit our website for other great titles: www.newleafpress.com

For information regarding author interviews,
please contact the publicity department at (870) 438-5288.

New Leaf Press
A Division of New Leaf Publishing Group
www.newleafpress.com

Contents

Introduction

A lady approached me at a conference recently, picked up a copy of one of my books, and asked, "Is this book focused more on the 'big picture,' or is it 'practical and how-to'?" I told her it was both but that it focused more on the macro-view, with micro-application. She said, "Oh, I'm not interested then. I don't care why my child behaves the way he does, I just want something that will fix the problem." I tried to explain to her that we will approach treatment differently based on what we believe is causing the problem. If our child's leg hurts, it matters drastically whether he or she has broken a bone or been stung by a wasp. Giving him or her a tranquilizer may numb the pain, but the cause really does make a difference.

After some conversation, I told her, "The way you describe what you are looking for makes me think of someone who is obsessed with knowing how to drive a new car. They want to learn about the wipers, the radio, the brakes, the windows, the seat controls, and the rearview mirror. Finally, they say, 'I have this car figured out! I'm ready to drive!' We may ask, 'Where are you going?' to which they may reply, 'Oh, that doesn't matter. I just want to drive. It doesn't matter where.' " For me, as a parent, destination is of utmost importance. Eternity in heaven with my Lord and Savior is the goal that I have for each of my ten children. It matters very much where this car is headed.

In this book, I will be focusing primarily on the big picture. I believe parenting is a lot like a thousand-piece puzzle. Most parents have the pieces all spread out on the table; they just need help putting them together. They know a lot of Bible verses, but they don't have a biblical theology of parenting. It's my ambition to show them the box top.

I'm going to shoot straight with you right from the beginning. The book that most parents need is not the one they are looking for.

Most parents want a book that will "fix their child" in three easy steps, in 30 days (or less). While understandable, this expectation is wrongheaded and will never work. The problem lies far more with us, the parents, than it does with our child. If we don't understand that truth, we will only remain frustrated and disappointed with our child.

Jesus explained the situation this way:

> Can a blind man lead a blind man? Will they not both fall into a pit? A disciple is not above his teacher, but everyone when he is fully trained will be like his teacher. Why do you see the speck that is in your brother's eye, but do not notice the log that is in your own eye? How can you say to your brother, 'Brother, let me take out the speck that is in your eye,' when you yourself do not see the log that is in your own eye? You hypocrite, first take the log out of your own eye, and then you will see clearly to take out the speck that is in your brother's eye (Luke 6:39b–42).

Parenting is discipleship. Your child is learning from you. You are the teacher. Far more is caught than taught in parenting. Children listen to what you say, but they watch how you live. When you are slack in dealing with character issues in your own life, it short circuits your ability to effectively reach your child's heart. You can be so focused on helping your child with his or her speck that you don't realize he or she is tuning you out because all the child can see is the beam protruding from your own proverbial eye. Like it or not, the problem is almost always with us, not ultimately with our children.

The far greater need is to fundamentally change our own hearts and minds as parents. As a principle, that simply MUST happen before any change will come for our youth. But authors know that suggesting the parent is the one who needs to change the most is offensive to most readers. Books that focus more on the parent than the child aren't popular and won't sell well. So, such books go unwritten. Instead, we have lots of "cheerleader" books that tell you what a great job you are doing. Or titles full of behavior modification techniques that are supposed to train our children to have good manners. With enough tips, tricks, and methods, it is believed we can modify our child's behavior to become socially acceptable. Perhaps we can learn the perfect approach to timeouts, or some magic cure that will solve bickering, sibling rivalry, laziness, backtalking, media addiction, lying, stealing, bad attitudes, apathy, angry outbursts, rebellion, inattention, or any other number of "fruits" that annoy, inconvenience, and embarrass us. Sadly, most books focus on trimming the branches and never really get to the heart of the matter (the roots). Therefore, even after the parent has finished reading the popular parenting book, all the behavioral issues in the children stay the same (or get worse) despite lots of pontification on the topic.

This book will not flail at branches but will take an axe to the heart of the real problem. While recognizing there is great value in science and brain research, this book presupposes that your child is more than mere neurons firing in a random universe (only to be understood and treated biologically). Your child is a complex being made up of body, mind, soul, and spirit. Every facet of the complete person needs to be evaluated and understood.

It is my belief that the Bible is not merely a group of moral lessons or philosophical ideas. I believe it is the inspired, inerrant, infallible, timeless Word of God. When we read the Bible, it should be understood as being the revealed truth of God Himself.

> For the word of God is living and active, sharper than any two-edged sword, piercing to the division of soul and of spirit, of joints and of marrow, and discerning the thoughts and intentions of the heart (Heb. 4:12).

> Knowing this first of all, that no prophecy of Scripture comes from someone's own interpretation. For no prophecy was ever produced by the will of man, but men spoke from God as they were carried along by the Holy Spirit (2 Pet. 1:20–21).

If the revealed Word of God is not your starting point, you will be very frustrated with this book. I will be using a lot of Scripture because I believe God knows better than you and me.

My wife, Brook, and I, at the time of this writing, have ten children (five boys and five girls) ranging in age from 19 years to nine months. We currently have four teenagers still living at home (although our oldest is now working full-time outside our home). So, we get a lot of opportunity to put into practice what I will be talking to you about in this book. But despite all of the experience we have had in our own parenting journey, and despite having some great mentors who have taught us (many that I consider to be true experts on parenting), I believe that we really have no wisdom or insights that will be beneficial to you. The Apostle Paul said, "For I know that nothing good dwells in me, that is, in my flesh" (Rom. 7:18a). The only wisdom we have, we received from God.

> Every good gift and every perfect gift is from above. . . (James 1:17).

> For who sees anything different in you? What do you have that you did not receive? If then you received it, why do you boast as if you did not receive it? (1 Cor. 4:7).

It is our desire to impart to you the wisdom that is from above, not worldly humanistic wisdom (see 1 Cor. 3:19 and James 3:15).

> And I was with you in weakness and in fear and much trembling, and my speech and my message were not in plausible words of wisdom, but in demonstration of the Spirit and of power, so that your faith might not rest in the wisdom of men but in the power of God.

> Yet among the mature we do impart wisdom, although it is not a wisdom of this age or of the rulers of this age, who are doomed to pass away. But we impart a secret and hidden wisdom of God, which God decreed before the ages for our glory (1 Cor. 2:3–7).

Oftentimes, God's wisdom seems counter-intuitive and backward to the way we would be inclined to think. We tend to foolishly rely on our own understanding (see Prov. 3:5–7). The Bible says, "There is a way that seems right to a man, but its end is the way to death" (Prov. 14:12). We want no part of that ungodly wisdom that will shipwreck our marriages and result in our children floundering in life. We need something solid, stable, and trustworthy. We don't want to build our houses on the shifting sand of popular opinion, trends, fads, and pop psychology (see Matt. 7:24–27). We want to build our family on the rock of Christ Jesus (our only sure foundation).

This will seem foolish to many who do not have the Spirit of Christ within them. Spiritual things are spiritually discerned (and you need to have God's Spirit living in you to do that).

> Now we have received not the spirit of the world, but the Spirit who is from God, that we might understand the things freely given us by God. And we impart this in words not taught by human wisdom but taught by the Spirit, interpreting spiritual truths to those who are spiritual. The natural person does not accept the things of the Spirit of God, for they are folly to him, and he is not able to understand them because they are spiritually discerned (1 Cor. 2:12–14).

At this point, some of you will want to bail out on this book, and we understand that. There are lots of other books out there that will teach you how to count to three, hold your breath, snap your wrist with a rubber band, and hand out stickers as a way to change your rebellious child. But if you care enough to risk having to make changes in your own way of thinking and living, then let's walk together on this path of learning to parent our children after the ways of God.

As we move forward, I (Israel) will be doing the bulk of the writing. Brook's input has permeated this entire manuscript, even if it is in my voice. When Brook is speaking uniquely, it will be specified in the text.

Chapter 1

Losing a Generation

Baby Boomers and the Jesus Movement

I grew up in the 1980s in the Evangelical church culture. At the time, baby boomers (those born from 1946–1964) were recognizing the mistakes their parents had made by being so career-driven and focused on material gain. The boomers rejected their parents' values in the 1960s, and many of them became the "hippie" generation. They threw convention to the wind and became wild young adults, embracing free love, drugs, social protests, and rock and roll. Their excessive hedonistic lifestyles (seeking mainly pleasure and temporal satisfaction) created a lot of emptiness and regret that haunted them (especially in their later years when they became parents).

In the 1970s, God moved powerfully among that generation in what sociologists now call "The Jesus Movement." It was an authentic move of God that led many of these hippies to find faith in Christ. While they were the most unlikely candidates to ever end up in church, many of these folks got married, held steady jobs, and eventually became "the establishment." As parents, they wanted a different life for their children, but they often didn't know how to best direct the next generation against the foolish choices they made in their own youth. As an antidote to their childhood with no boundaries, some of them looked for highly rigid structures that were rule-based and formulaic for their children. Legalism is an easy trap for some parents to fall into.

Many boomers were raised in non-Christian homes or merely nominal ones where church attendance was erratic and happened mostly on Christmas and Easter. When these folks got saved, they had a radical encounter (an experience) with Jesus that was real and genuine. The problem is that they weren't taught how to effectively disciple their children. Most of them assumed that the church would do it. Or they prayed that God would somehow "zap" their child with the Holy Ghost and they would just "get it."

Seventy Percent of Churched Youth Fall Away

Unfortunately, the data is in, and the "formula-based" or "hope-they-figure-it-out" approaches did not work. In fact, they failed miserably. In the first quarter of the twenty-first century, we have found young people leaving the faith of their parents in massive numbers. There are many studies on this mass exodus from church conducted by groups like Barna Research Group, America's Research Group, Pew Research, Nehemiah Institute, the Southern Baptist Council on Family Life, the Gen2 Survey, and others. Nearly all of them state that 60–88% (a consistent average of 70%) of all churched youth leave the church before they graduate from high school!

To make matters worse, of those few who make it through high school with their faith intact, an additional 70% will deny their Christian faith before the end of their freshman year at a secular college or university.[1]

If you look at biblical worldview, it is even worse! According to the Barna Group, "The research data showed that one pattern emerged loud and clear: young adults rarely possess a biblical worldview. The current study found that less than one-half of one percent of adults in the Mosaic generation – i.e., those aged 18 to 23 – have a biblical worldview."[2]

This is a scary prospect for the future of the Christian church in the West. Churches all over Europe and North America are closing. Church buildings, in places where the fires of the Reformation burned brightest, are now empty. They are being bought up by

---

1. From a study by CampusRenewal.org, https://onenewsnow.com/church/2017/08/13/ministries-tackle-70-rate-of-college-students-leaving-faith.
2. https://www.barna.com/research/barna-survey-examines-changes-in-worldview-among-christians-over-the-past-13-years/.

liquor stores, antique malls, and museums. Surely this grieves the heart of our Lord! When this scenario plays out in our own families, it is not merely statistics — it's devastating.

What Can We Do?

If we hope to turn the tide and see the effective discipleship of our youth, we are going to have to return to a gospel-centered approach to parenting. We will need to shake ourselves loose from the humanistic reasoning of our age and dare to think and act biblically. It has been said that to keep trying the same methods that have proven to fail and expecting different results is a definition of insanity.

We need to develop a theology of parenting. I believe the Bible speaks authoritatively to every sector of life. The good news for us is that Scripture is not silent on this issue. We don't need to be left uncertain in a world that seeks to submerge our families in its influence. God's Word contains everything we need to live godly lives.

> His divine power has granted to us all things that pertain to life and godliness, through the knowledge of him who called us to his own glory and excellence (2 Pet. 1:3).

Before we begin to put the pieces back together, let's back up, get a 30,000-foot view, and see where things began to go wrong for the Christian family. Knowing how things broke down in American society will help us be better equipped to avoid making toxic mistakes as we move forward into the future.

Chapter 2

The Battle for the Family

Hear, my son, your father's instruction, and forsake
not your mother's teaching (Prov. 1:8).

Although it is never objectively accurate to say that a certain time
period was "the good old days," there are many positive values that
our society has lost in the past 150 years. One of the most tragic of
these losses was the disintegration of the family culture, especially
multi-generational connections and legacies.

Because many of us have never experienced the benefits of the
family culture in our lifetimes, we may not even recognize our collective loss. Imagine with me, if you can, a culture where you are
surrounded with people who know and love you. There are parents, uncles and aunts, cousins, grandparents, and even on occasion
great-grandparents. Living, working, playing, and worshiping with
these loved ones creates a wonderful sense of security and stability.
You know who you are, to a great extent, because of your relationships with your surrounding family. Family can serve as a fixed reference point, linking you to geography and the past in a way no
other friendship or community can.

Allow me to outline some of the paradigm shifts that have
occurred in American culture over the past 150 years. They have
brought about a disconnected and individualistic society that has
replaced the previous family-centered culture.

The Breakdown of the Family Culture

I would say that the breakdown of the family culture in America
began largely after the Civil War in 1865. Over 620,000 American

men died in a war that left virtually every family missing a loved one. In the Reconstruction that followed, men and women often left their homes and began to work in factories, taking advantage of the new breakthroughs of invention and industry. Prior to the Civil War, most Americans were agrarian. Rural families worked on farms or owned family businesses.

The Industrial Revolution

At the turn of the twentieth century, it became clear that the machine was the way of the future. From Eli Whitney's cotton gin to Henry Ford's automobile, from the steam engine to the success of the Wright Brothers' flying machine, people were finding faster and more efficient ways to do everything, including get around.

Wise families started their own businesses and hired family members to keep their income "in house." Around the turn of the twentieth century, many families became famous for developing financial systems that grew the family wealth exponentially. The Rockefellers, Vanderbilts, Studebakers, the J.P. Morgan family, and later the Kennedys, are all examples of family wealth. Whether you admire or disdain that kind of economic nepotism, you must admit they knew the collective potential of the family culture. For most families, however, mass production and factory labor took at least one parent (usually the father) away from the home into the "workforce."

Government Education

In 1852, Horace Mann had established the first government-controlled, compulsory attendance school system in Massachusetts. This model spread around the country, and before long, not only was the father removed from the home, but the children were as well. Instead of working alongside their parents, receiving an education through family enterprise (and supplemented with either homeschooling or formal academics in a community-controlled, parent-directed educational co-op), students were now enrolled in "assembly-line" educational factories utilizing the same modernistic principles that were revolutionizing every other industry.

More important than the physical separation that occurred through mandatory governmental education was the emotional distance that was experienced as children embraced the culture of "social education." Friendships through the "peer group" replaced the family as the child's primary, foundational relationship.

Women's Liberation

Eventually, the twentieth century "Feminist Movement" put most mothers into the workplace as well, effectively removing the central hub of the family from the home. Mothers were convinced to leave the education of their children to trained and certified "experts." With the additional tax burden placed on families because of state-funded schools and other ever-widening government-funded social programs, many families felt the need to have two incomes just to make ends meet. There is no way to estimate the effect that the so-called "Women's Liberation" movement has had on the lives of millions of children. Children need both parents (ideally) to be emotionally and socially balanced, but they especially need the daily nurturing of their mothers.

While some point to the positive gains made through equal rights movements like Women's Liberation, the "freeing" of women from their families has devastated the family culture. Women's Liberation mainly "freed" women from their children and made them slaves to their jobs. It's not merely a matter of men and women working a job outside of the home; it is a mindset shift from parents being responsible for the care and nurturing of their own offspring to an expectation that the government is supposed to provide for all of our needs from the cradle to the grave, and we all work to support an overgrown bureaucracy that seeks to do for us what we should be doing for ourselves.

Mass distribution of the birth control pill in 1950 further liberated women from children, encouraging them to limit their family size to one or two children. Daycares began to spring up in order to allow mothers to place babies who were only a few weeks old into the hands of unknown caretakers. Increasingly, family life was sacrificed on the altar of economic pursuits. This has become the overwhelming trend in most of Europe and Asia as well. Many nations have fallen behind the 2.1 childbirth ratio needed to keep a society economically viable, and they have slipped into economic recession. There are more senior citizens to care for and not enough wage earners (or family members who care) to provide for them. The United States has a current birth rate of 1.73 children per household (in 2018)[1] and is the only nation in the world that is losing population by birth but gaining by immigration. In the long run, such an approach is not economically viable and will cause a national economic collapse.

Mass Transportation

Mass transportation had a massive impact on reshaping American families. As new economic opportunities beckoned, families uprooted from the old home place and took off across the country. The railroad, and later the automobile and the airplane, gave people a mobility that changed the landscape of America. Since the telegraph, and eventually the telephone, allowed families to keep in touch over the miles, many families made the choice to exchange local relationships with their extended families for distance ones. This geographical distance removed economic interdependence and thereby removed a primary reason for staying connected. Working together for a common goal is great cement to bond relationships.

Shifting from a "Folk Culture" to a "Popular (Pop) Culture"

America quickly shifted from a "Folk Culture" (where people grew up in a close-knit community and had a producer mentality) to a "Pop Culture" (where individualists worked to earn enough money to purchase entertainment). Rather than producing bluegrass music on the porch with friends and neighbors (with instruments we made ourselves), we now isolate ourselves from others, listening on our earbuds to music we downloaded from the Internet. Art was no longer something we produced in communal relationships (like the old quilting circles); it became a commodity we would buy. This shift in thinking from being creative to being passive sponges of information has been devastating to our culture.

Mass Media and the Creation of a Mass Culture

With the advent of radio and eventually television, all Americans, regardless of their geography, had access to the same news

---

1. https://www.cdc.gov/nchs/data/vsrr/vsrr-007-508.pdf.

and information. Mass media and standardized education helped to shape a general culture. Rather than localized, provincial folk or agrarian cultures (that informed your views and values), Americans were increasingly adopting the mass ideas of corporate advertising and government propaganda. Regardless of your geography, you were watching the same television shows, hearing the same commercials, and using the same textbooks as everyone else in America.

What's the Big Deal?

To some, none of this is important. If the values of the current popular trends have already become your own, then who cares about all this cultural distinctiveness and familial identity? Who cares about the family culture and being connected to the generations who precede and follow you? Who cares about ensuring mechanisms of restraint, accountability, responsibility, and obligation within the larger family context? Who cares about passing on values from your children to their children and to generations who have not yet been born?

If these values are not important to you, then rest assured that your task is easy. All you need to do is absolutely nothing in order to ensure that your children will embrace whatever cultural trends happen to be hip at the moment. If you want your children to grow up to love only themselves, think only of themselves, see no obligation to their parents or grandparents, make all of their major life choices with no regard for how it impacts their extended families, or to be simply users and consumers rather than creative producers and artisans, then your task is very easy indeed. Just do nothing as hard as you can. Send your children to any local government school, let them grow up with their little brains saturated in television, video games, and other multimedia, and never, ever encourage them to build, read books, dream, play outside, have discussions with their gray-headed relatives, or see themselves as part of a family unit. Raising one more self-absorbed, media-gorged, financially irresponsible individual who feels no responsibility outside him or herself is very easy indeed. Just follow the cultural current.

Our Mission (Should We Choose to Accept It)

It takes work to pass on family values. It takes work to maintain family relationships. It takes work to think in terms of a multi-generational vision. For me, the work is worth it.

I don't want to merely curse the darkness. We can't turn back the clock and become Amish (although I'm sure I'd enjoy that — about 60% of the time!). Perhaps we can find creative ways to use technology and communication tools to keep us together rather than to split us apart. Maybe we can find ways to live in this twenty-first century without being absorbed in the narcissism of it all. Perhaps we can keep the positive and enduring values of the generations past while enjoying the comforts and conveniences of our modern age. The one thing I can assure you, however, is that strong family bonds and the transmission of the right kinds of values never happen by accident. It takes intentionality, focus, planning, and a lot of hard work. Let's learn from the lessons of the past and seek to shine a light for future generations.

Chapter 3

Techno-Parenting

What has been is what will be, and what has been
done is what will be done, and there is nothing new
under the sun (Eccles. 1:9).

Leaving the Industrial Revolution and entering the digital age, we
find a new set of circumstances that threaten to tear the family apart.
The sad thing is that we have all welcomed this potential enemy into
our homes. In fact, we pay a lot of money to let it live in our homes.

Writing on technology is a bit tricky. Whenever you use the term
"technology," you immediately date your writing. I mean, if you pick
up a magazine talking about how wonderful a new 8-track player is,
you immediately know something about the age of the article. (I'd
go so far as to say if you even know what an 8-track player is, you
are showing your age!) In case you are wondering how I know about
them, I uh . . . I uh, saw one in a museum once! Heh, heh.

However, I have concluded that technology and the family
must be addressed. We will see more technological changes in the
next few decades than entire centuries in history have observed. Sci-
entists (and computer developers in particular) are on the verge of
technological breakthroughs we can barely fathom. Computers and
satellites have revolutionized nearly every industry. Political experts,
educators, and market specialists all agree that a student growing up
in the twenty-first century without basic computer skills will not be
able to compete in the ever-changing global economy.

I hope this study will expand our thinking and cause us to
follow more closely the will of our Savior in this matter. The focus

of this discussion will deal primarily with the Internet since I believe it is the form of technology that has the greatest implications for families today and in the future. It is a method of communication that many parents simply don't know how to harness.

What Is Good About Technology?

In my estimation, one of the fundamental purposes of technology should ultimately be to enhance the production of goods and services. We live in what is known as an "information age," and much of the Internet exists to host millions of pages of "content" and "information" for viewers to read and download.

Information is a good means, but it is a terrible end. To quote the wisdom of the Apostle Paul in his letter to the Corinthians, " 'knowledge' puffs up" (1 Cor. 8:1b). If the Internet is to endure as anything other than a virtual escape from reality, or a bastion of hedonistic pleasure and entertainment, it must help us produce better goods and services or live better lives. Information in a vacuum is useless (or destructive). It must help us do something better or make our lives easier in some way.

Of course, the truly astute will point out that this very book is information-based and that I am using words to question the endless use of words. Yes, but I trust that the Lord will use the ideas in this book to help you disciple your children or to bring your family closer together. It does serve a utilitarian purpose. Any good form of technology will enhance and improve what God has called us to do with our lives.

As a means of communication, the Internet can and should be used for evangelism, building up and equipping the saints for ministry, and providing businesses with more effective means of producing or marketing their goods and services. I'm not implying that everyone needs to use the Internet, but those who do should use it wisely for the Lord. "And whatever you do, in word or deed, do everything in the name of the Lord Jesus, giving thanks to God the Father through him" (Col. 3:17).

Amusing Ourselves to Death

Much of technology exists as a vehicle for entertainment. Computers and television are largely used by American children to play games or to enjoy entertaining shows. I certainly have nothing against relaxing and taking a break, presupposing, of course, that we are living purposeful lives where rest is peripheral and serving is central. We need to have something to rest from, after all. How do you rest from being lazy? Yet, it does bother me that today's youth are, as Neil Postman (author of *Technopoly*) puts it, "amusing themselves to death." Being entertained is not something that many American teenagers "do" so much as who they "are." It seems that popular culture and media expect teens to exist as sponges to be filled with the expensive content (no matter how useless) of whatever music or programming they wish to propagate.

Technology has an addictive nature. It is very easy to become hooked on it, almost like a narcotic. Entertainment is often used for the same reasons that most people use drugs or any addictive substance: to pursue pleasure and to relieve pain.

Many people entertain themselves because they want to feel good and enjoy themselves or because they have a deep emotional void that they are trying to fill. They want to abandon themselves in a "virtual reality" and forget about the harshness of the life they are trapped in. People who are entertained for these reasons are liable to escape not only from reality, but from reason as well. It is when we are in a passive consumerist mindset that we are most prone to ingesting harmful ideas and worldviews imbedded in the media we consume.

Technology as a Tool

Biblically speaking, neither technology usage nor entertainment are mandatory moral imperatives. In regard to having children use technology in their education, I would strongly admonish you to consider the following: "What call has God placed on your child's life, and what forms of technology will help your child achieve success in what God has called him or her to do?"

For example, if you believe that the Lord is drawing your child into a career as a chemist, by all means, utilize the appropriate technology available in that field. Microscopes, computer research, testing equipment, etc., will all be a part of fulfilling God's purpose in your young child's life. However, if your child is going to be an organic gardener, he or she will probably benefit more from books, mentoring, and getting his or her hands dirty than by buying expensive computer equipment. For those of you who do organic gardening and surf the web as well, if you can use technology to help you become a better gardener, then I propose that you do so (for the glory of God). I just question sometimes how much of what we do with computers and electronic gadgets makes us more efficient and effective and how much of it slows us down and hinders our usefulness for God's Kingdom.

To illustrate the point, I'm going to resort to the realm of the ridiculous for a moment. Let's say that you have a construction worker who buys a new framing hammer and is totally infatuated with it. While his co-workers are busy putting up a house, he sits at the job site admiring his new "waffle head." He has made the mistake of viewing his hammer as the chief end as opposed to it being a tool that enables him to build the house, which is the ultimate goal.

Many folks view the Internet or television in the same way. They admire the tool and see it as a necessary good simply because it exists and they like it. The fact is that all media are "educational." We need to make sure we are being educated in beneficial things.

What About Online Education?

Doing studies online is a trendy choice with many homeschooling parents nowadays. It frees mothers up to do other tasks, and it can provide special tutelage for students struggling with, or wanting to advance in, a specific subject. There are some definite advantages to multimedia and online learning. However, you also should consider the drawbacks. A few of the advantages include audio/visual effects that bring to life events and concepts and an interactive interface that allows computer courses to hold the attention of the student who tends to daydream. Being proficient in basic computer skills can help young people be ready for future employment opportunities. Benefits for the parents can include outsourced grading services and less time spent managing actual instruction.

I guess my greatest concern about online and computer education is that it can become a substitute for parents. In order to be effective parents for our children, we need to be there — engaged and engaging, participating and calling our children to participate. Because our main goal is discipleship, we should be more concerned with relationships and winning the hearts of our children than we are with teaching academic concepts. A computer or another teacher online or via video can, perhaps, teach our children just as well or better than we can, but are we sure that is the approach we want to take? I am not opposed to supplementing education with multimedia — I think it can be very beneficial — but I am against replacing parental involvement with an impersonal machine.

Especially when children are young, they should be learning their values from their parents. You can give your child a book on a computer, but it will never replace the closeness developed by having that youngster crawl onto your lap, rest his or her head against you, and listen to you read a story. Your children know you are investing of yourself for them, and that teaches a lesson they will never forget. It just isn't the same to snuggle up next to a computer screen.

We don't want to develop children who know how to relate to a machine but who fail to spend adequate time with their family or friends. I know some children who can spend hours at a time playing electronic games. If you walk into the room where they are playing, they don't even see you (or, if they do, they are so rude and antisocial they ignore you and pretend you aren't there). There are social skills such as being polite, learning to converse with people of all age levels, and developing friendships that simply cannot be learned adequately in the virtual world.

Producers Versus Consumers

I constantly tell my children, "There are two kinds of people in the world: consumers and producers." While we are all consumers, we want to be defined predominately by producing more than we consume. Creativity is about making art. Entertainment is about buying and passively consuming someone else's creation. So much of pop culture exists to create dissatisfaction with what we have and to foster an insatiable fixation with the newest, latest, hippest, fastest, and coolest. This is contrary to the teachings of the Bible.

> But godliness with contentment is great gain, for we brought nothing into the world, and we cannot

take anything out of the world. But if we have food and clothing, with these we will be content (1 Tim. 6:6–8).

Contentment is not laziness but a satisfaction with whatever God enables us to be able to produce and achieve.

Striving to Rest

I know I probably sound extremely utilitarian at this point. Some of you may be thinking, "Doesn't this guy believe in fun? Are we never to play games or enjoy life?" I believe in rest and renewal, but I think there are some general scriptural guidelines that apply. We need to be purposeful in our resting. There is a tendency to "veg out" when we are emotionally or physically wasted, but this can be dangerous. Especially when our body and mind are weak, it is not very wise to indiscriminately give ourselves over to mindless input. It was during one of these "veg-out" sessions that King David gave his heart over to a lustful, illicit relationship with Bathsheba (2 Sam. 11).

The Word instructs us: "Be still before the LORD and wait patiently for him" (Ps. 37:7a). Does your screen/technology use help or hinder your ability to wait patiently on the Lord?

"But know that the LORD has set apart the godly for himself. . . . ponder in your own hearts on your beds, and be silent. Selah" (Ps. 4:3–4). Does technology help you to slow down to ponder the ways of the Lord?

"Be still, and know that I am God" (Ps. 46:10a). When is the last time you took 30 minutes to simply be still and do nothing?

". . . aspire to live quietly" (1 Thess. 4:11a). Does your family ever have times when everyone is awake and intentionally being quiet?

In our day and age, it is a struggle to rest. Electronic input is not always restful; it is often stressful. If the only way we know to unwind is by turning on noise or by watching a screen, I would venture to say we are addicted to technology. I believe most working Americans today struggle with some sort of attention-deficit problem.

"FOMO" (Fear of Missing Out) is a driving force that causes many of us to check our smartphone incessantly to see if we got an online message or if someone commented on our social media post. There is so much that competes for our notice. Distractions in the form of advertisements abound. The goal is to entice us to buy more, consume more, and be constantly dissatisfied. I believe the enemy of our souls desires for us to be so busy that we have no time to be quiet and still before our Lord. Satan will even settle for "Christian" entertainment if that is what it takes to pull us away from God. You see, it is only in those quiet moments that we say, "Search me, O God, and know my heart! Try me and know my thoughts! And see if there be any grievous way in me, and lead me in the way everlasting!" (Ps. 139:23–24).

"For God alone, O my soul, wait in silence, for my hope is from him" (Ps. 62:5).

It is hard work to clear our minds of temporal, earthly things and focus on the truly significant. It is a discipline to lay aside the "tyranny of the urgent." As the writer of Hebrews says, "Let us therefore strive to enter that rest, so that no one may fall by the same sort of disobedience" (Heb. 4:11). Our Savior said, "Come to me, all who labor and are heavy laden, and I will give you rest. Take my yoke upon you, and learn from me, for I am gentle and lowly in heart, and you will find rest for your souls. For my yoke is easy, and my burden is light" (Matt. 11:28–30).

Even in our rest and relaxation, we are to turn to Jesus. We must not allow anything to pull our eyes away from Him. I'm not suggesting a kind of pietism that removes us from anything that is earthly to embrace only the "spiritual."

> This is what I mean, brothers: the appointed time has grown very short. From now on, let those who have wives live as though they had none, and those who mourn as though they were not mourning, and those who rejoice as though they were not rejoicing, and those who buy as though they had no goods, and those who deal with the world as though they had no dealings with it. For the present form of this world is passing away. I want you to be free from anxieties (1 Cor. 7:29–32a).

The best way to be free from concern is to use the things of earth for the Kingdom of God. We must not allow them to hinder our pursuit of Him. Even in our rest and relaxation, we should use those times to be renewed and refueled for Kingdom work. Jesus enjoyed times of relaxation with family and friends, but His life was characterized by His focused devotion to the purpose of the Father.

Content and Form

There are two important factors that must be included in this discussion. We need to evaluate the content (information) transmitted through technology and the form itself (the vehicle that is utilized to send the information). I find that Christians are much more equipped to evaluate the content of various media than they are to understand potential destructive elements in the form or the means of communication. For example, it is easy to denounce a website that promotes immorality as being unfit for use in the Christian home. However, do we think critically about the vehicle (the Internet) that brings that website to us?

Christians are sometimes rightfully concerned about the number of curse words or sexual scenes in a movie, but how many consider how beneficial most movies or television shows are in general? Even if a show is acceptable, is it worthwhile?

The Medium Is the Message

Are there negative aspects to the forms of technology that we should question? Obviously, we don't want our children playing video or computer games where violence and cruelty are encouraged. But can the process of playing the games themselves be harmful? Michael Medved (author of the book *Hollywood vs. America*) has said that the problem with television is not only the violence, profanity, and sexual content — it is just too much TV!

For example, there are physical considerations to spending inordinate time before a monitor. Watching TV, playing video games, or typing on a computer can all have harmful side effects to our minds and bodies. We can develop eye strain, become overweight, or develop poor physique from lack of exercise. Some medical doctors are concerned about neck injuries from people looking down at their phones all the time. We might get carpal tunnel syndrome from typing too much, we may develop various stress-related illnesses or headaches, etc. We shouldn't become paranoid, of course, but we should be aware that the *content* of technology is not the only destructive element. Too much time on computers and television can have harmful side effects even if we are only viewing good content.

Why Limit Children's Screen Time? (Brook)

If you are like me, you've got a to-do list a mile long, and you need a little space of time when your young crew is safely occupied. Enter screen time, the new wonder drug! It is like having a free babysitter.

But it soon becomes the convenience we need to distract them when we're waiting at the airport instead of the slow, methodical memory games our grandparents taught us ("I went to Grandma's attic and I got . . ." or "I spy with my little eye . . .") that employed memory use, observation, and lots of giggles as the game took an unexpected turn. Long lines at the grocery store, where a child waiting with his parents became an exercise in counting nearby displays or conversing quietly with a sibling, have been replaced with screen time to escape the torture of waiting. Potty training, which used to take long hours of sitting with our child — explaining, talking, reading, singing — has reached a new era where we stick a screen in our toddler's hands so we don't have to wrestle through their wait.

When life, in the natural course of things, brings waiting, boredom, and unpleasant circumstances, our culture increasingly wants to hand a screen to the little ones to "medicate" them. Because, frankly, their impatience isn't convenient . . . for us. These small ones become noisy, fidgety, and grumpy, and it is easy to just turn a favorite game app on and let them have at it.

I'm an introvert. In order to recharge, I like some quiet. That's good and fine in its rightful place, but the human desire for a good thing needs to be kept in check when something of greater value hangs in the balance. Perhaps you are like me and you're looking for the quiet button on your child. We need to beware as parents that we keep things in balance by not escaping for our own me time when our children need a real live parent to interact and engage, lead and love.

In order to regain some peace in the home, parents often stuff a screen in their child's face when the youngster misbehaves. It's a wonder drug! Sibling rivalry seems cut off at the pass when brothers and sisters are split up and sent to different ends of the house with a screen to calm down. Angry outbursts, demands made in the toy store, and rude and ugly comments are all dispelled by the eye-candy on the screen. When we give a child this kind of diversion, we are only buying for ourselves a few moments of quiet. In the long run, however, we are stealing from our children the time and help they need to process through the emotions and problems in their lives. I'd suggest that this exchange is unhealthy.

When we buy this kind of peace, we are only delaying the inevitable outburst of ugly heart issues. Diverting a child's attention does nothing to mend sibling relationships or to help them process the need for self-control. It is my observation that constantly re-directing children from the (difficult!) processes of taking personal responsibility, of boredom, of repentance where necessary, or of basically anything dealing with real-life situations breeds escalated anger. The root issues aren't addressed, and the next time the situation repeats itself, we're surprised to see the child's reactions are only stronger. The real emotion diffuser comes when a child is shown how to rein in his or her own actions and is led to the Lord for the power to do so.

The Dark Side of the Net (Israel)

Under the heading of harmful "content," I would list the obvious: pornography, violence, new age or occult propaganda, paranormal activity, profanity, and on and on. As the Apostle Paul says, "Now the works of the flesh are evident" (Gal. 5:19a).

While these things are generally clear to most Christians, there is an insidiousness about "the net" that has a real potential of ensnaring us. They don't call it a "web" for no reason! Let's look at a few of the pitfalls for Christian families using the Internet.

Unauthorized Relationships

I have seen families, who I believed were devout and seeking the Lord, totally shipwrecked by allowing unchecked technology into their homes. Many will argue that there were obviously already "heart" problems in place and that technology had nothing to do with the spiritual demise of these folks. I know that just as technology can be a tool for good, it can also be used by the enemy as a tool of destruction. No, we can't blame the tool exclusively, but it does play a part. Just as a teenager who commits murder after hundreds of hours of listening to music containing violent lyrics or playing violent video games cannot blame the songs or the games, it is ludicrous to say that what we input into our lives will never come out. "For as he thinks in his heart, so is he" (Prov. 23:7a; NKJV).

You become the sum of what you fill your life with. What you fill your life with will overflow when you get bumped. If you have filled your life with the influences of the world, worldliness will pour out of your life. If you have filled your life with the spirit of Christ, His nature and character will be revealed when you are tested.

I personally know three families who declare the Name of Jesus yet have gone through a divorce after an adulterous relationship developed online. In two of the cases, it was the women who "fell in love" with men they met in discussion groups. In the third, a man met another woman hundreds of miles away who he thought fulfilled his dreams. He left his wife and two children to move across the country to be with his new lover. The two women were homeschooling moms with many children, and the man was a fellow with whom I had been in a Bible study at my church.

The Apostle Paul warned of people who get into the habit of going from house to house: "Besides that, they learn to be idlers, going about from house to house, and not only idlers, but also gossips and busybodies, saying what they should not. So I would have younger widows marry, bear children, manage their households, and give the adversary no occasion for slander" (1 Tim. 5:13–14). You can go from "house to house" via the Internet without ever leaving home. What may seem like harmless "chatting" online can be the tool the enemy uses to ruin our homes.

Unprofitable Relationships

My wife pointed out to me that not only are unauthorized relationships a problem on the web, but unprofitable ones are as well. As usual, I think she has a good point! Some people chat to others online because they need a support group. That isn't necessarily bad, but sometimes spiritual needs cannot be met by the virtual community.

Regardless of what we may think, virtual friendships are simply not as good as having someone to talk to face to face. An arm around the shoulder, a hand of friendship, and hearing the laughter of someone we love cannot be replaced by "LOL!" (an acronym for "laugh out loud"). As an aside: One lady who constantly saw people typing "LOL" in their emails assumed it stood for "lots of love." Seeing a good witnessing opportunity, she began ending all her correspondences with "Jesus died for you, LOL!" It helps to learn the terms if you are going to communicate online! This is another example of how true communication gets lost in the impersonal world of computers.

There are often local people and real relationships we are neglecting while we spend hours online debating with people we don't know about things that often don't matter in the grand scheme of things.

Pornography

While pornography is perhaps the most publicized "dark side" of the net, its potential for harm should not be underestimated. Having unfiltered Internet is like having an unfiltered sewer pipe running into your home. Many pornographic companies purposefully register religious and educational keywords with search engines to draw in children and religious people. So, your child might be doing educational research online and be led inadvertently to a page they never would have sought out.

"Sexting" with cell phones is a major problem with teenagers (and many adults). Many teens send each other inappropriate photos or sensual text messages, often without their parents knowing. One family told me that their 15-year-old son had nude photos of a girl from his church youth group. She had texted the photos to her boyfriend, who had sent them on to all his other male friends.

I would strongly encourage Christian families to use porn-blocking and accountability software. At present, we spend $16 a month for the program we use to cover all the devices used in our home.

Many offer various levels of parental controls. This will not completely eliminate access to all objectionable sites (there are just too many sites on the net), but in most cases, it will vastly reduce the risk of someone stumbling on something destructive by accident.

Because of the dangers of Internet porn, we do not allow our children to have Internet-enabled devices in their bedrooms, and they can use them only when allowed for constructive purposes in a public area where other responsible family members are present. We do not allow our young children to own handheld devices for their own personal use (they can borrow ours), and it is not assumed that teenagers will automatically get a smartphone. If they can't afford to pay for one, I'm of the opinion that they probably don't need one. I'm not going to dictate policy for your family — perhaps your teenager works a job or goes to school and needs one — but it is imperative to make a wise and informed decision about smartphone use and access and not just capitulate to what your young people and family may believe is "normal."

I heard a public school principal say that the right age to give your child a smartphone is the age when you feel your daughters can handle constant feelings of inferiority from social pressure and when you want your sons to start looking at porn. That sounds harsh, but that is his assessment based on what he sees in school every day. In the end, you are the parent. You need to decide what is best for your family.

Don't You Trust Me?

One charge that always gets leveled at parents who want to monitor their child's Internet/social media use is "Don't you trust me?!" The teenager expresses hurt at the suggestion that they would ever look at or do something inappropriate on the net. As parents, we need to lead by example here. Brook and I share passwords for all our phones, computers, and online accounts. As a father, I have Internet filtering and accountability software on every device I own that has online access. My wife has the password so I can't bypass it or turn it off. She receives updates on my media use and can track my online history. I am not asking my teenagers to submit to standards that I don't implement myself.

The fact is, none of us should trust ourselves. We don't have specific distrust in our child, but rather, we aren't naïve about human nature. We are to put "no confidence in the flesh" (see Phil. 3:3–4). None of us are above being tempted or sinning. We want to encourage a lifestyle of accountability and demonstrate it by our example. Our children will not likely embrace what we will not walk out. We are not to be accountable to our children, but to our spouses and accountability partners (allies). They are accountable to us, but we model such behavior by being accountable to spiritual mentors in our own lives.

Loss of Privacy

It seems the Internet is one of the most sophisticated information-gathering resources in the history of humankind. Companies store all sorts of data that they learn about visitors to their website. For example, if you place an order while shopping at an online store, it is likely that you will be greeted by name the next time you visit their site. You will be given an opportunity to choose from some pre-selected items they think you might be interested in buying based on your previous purchases. They build a database profile of you as a consumer and try to advertise to your specific interests and hobbies.

While that seems harmless enough (albeit somewhat unnerving and annoying), it simply points out how much everyone seems to know about us these days. We get phone calls at our homes from people we have never heard of trying to sell us things we don't want. How do they get our phone numbers, anyway? We place an order with an online company that promptly sells our email address to a dozen other companies that "spam" us with offers for everything under the sun. And, of course, there is always the age-old fear of the government spying on us for reasons unbeknownst to us. On the web, it seems that sinister criminals and maniacs, who develop viruses for fun, can maintain anonymity, but the rest of us become victims of our relentless information-glut society.

As mobile technology has increased, social media sites can virtually track our every move, every purchase, lifestyle habits, and beliefs. We are automatically "checked-in" to various businesses, and our every move is cataloged by the government, by businesses, and, in some cases, criminals who can stalk us or rob us blind, since they know we are not home (and where we are). As adults, it is our choice regarding how concerned we are with our privacy, but our youth often don't know the inherent dangers of giving personal and private information to strangers (who may be predators) online. They require our guidance.

Wasting Time and Internet Addiction

The interactive nature of the Internet has an addictive element. It is easy to plan to go online for 15 minutes and end up spending an hour surfing around looking at various websites. That is how the web is designed. Everything is vying for your attention, trying to get you to click a banner or link to take you to another site that promises an informative news brief, a sale on an item you have been wanting, or the opportunity to win some prize. The world is at your fingertips, and it is hard to discern when you should turn it off. We thrive on the constant boost of dopamine that gives us happy "feels" when we entertain ourselves online.

One homeschooling mom who was a regular on a homeschool discussion group online found that she was spending four hours per day chatting with other moms about how to be a better wife and mother! She had become addicted to chatting and was beginning to lie to her husband to explain why she hadn't accomplished anything during the day. She would tell him that she was sick and had to stay in bed to try to recover. Of course, this caused a double anxiety for the husband, who was concerned not only about the dishes and laundry piling up everywhere, but also about his "ailing" wife.

On a plane recently, I was talking with a young man from Dallas, Texas, who maintains a web server for his company. He spends at least 70 hours a week on the computer. He has five computers in his home, and he must check email every couple of hours or else he begins to panic. He was on his way to visit his mother in Nappanee, Indiana, where he had been raised. (Nappanee is known as a prominent Amish community.) I said, "Well, you will probably be glad to get away from computers for a week, won't you?" "Actually," he laughed, "my mom wants me to work on fixing her computer while

I'm there. And, I can check my email and work on our company's server from my mom's high-speed Internet line." I asked him if he thought he could go 48 hours without touching a computer. He admitted that he knew he couldn't.

Texting and posting on social media are a huge addiction for many people. One famous Hollywood marriage ended because the husband was so addicted to messaging on his phone that his wife said she couldn't take it anymore and left him!

At a recent parenting seminar, a couple took me aside after the event to ask my advice. They had a 19-year-old son who they said was addicted to video games. They said it took them a long time to even admit that fact and use the term "addiction." He did not work or study. He played video games almost constantly — over 12 hours a day. When the parents went to bed, he was still playing, so they had no idea how late he actually played. After much discussion and prayer, they decided to confront him. They told him they would be taking his video game console away. He retorted that they had given it to him as a gift and therefore had no right to take it back. The parents were guilt-ridden that they had purchased and encouraged the means of his addiction.

After consideration, they said they would not take the console away but that, as parents, they were stewards, before God, concerning what transpired under their roof. They could not allow him to continue to play his games. He became angry and said he would move out. They told him they did not wish for this to be the motive for why he moved out, but if he would not abide by their rules, that was his choice. So, he called his buddies and told them he would be moving into the apartment they all shared. When they told him what rent would cost, he admitted he could not pay it since he had no job.

Not to be dissuaded, he emptied his piggy bank, took his life savings (of $43 dollars), walked to Walmart, and bought a tent, which he pitched in his parents' backyard. The parents told me he had been living out there for the last three days. They didn't know what (or if) he was eating, and he only entered the house to use the restroom. He ran an extension cord from the back of their house into his tent and was gaming in his tent both day and night.

These Christian parents were heartbroken. They never wanted or anticipated this kind of outcome for their young adult. As with any addiction, it is appropriate for caring family members to seek intervention and appropriate professional therapy for those whose lives are controlled by negative habits.

Instant Gratification and Attention Deficit

As if Americans weren't impatient and stressed out enough, along comes the Internet with even greater promises of immediate satisfaction and fulfillment of every desire. (Next-day or same-day shipping has made our expectation for instant gratification even worse!) Children, who already lack the desire and natural ability to wait, may be encouraged to even more distraction, impatience, and lack of attention span by spending time online. An article in the December/January 2001 issue of *Publish* magazine details this point well. The author, Ilise Benun, says: .

> I am really impatient lately, much more than I have ever been. If I encounter a voice mail system while trying to make a phone call, I hang up. If there's a line at the bank, post office, or supermarket, I go somewhere else. I have no patience with friends who don't get to the point fast enough and, at a conference recently, I was literally in agony when one of the speakers dragged out his thoughts like a huge [electronic] file downloading.
>
> Speaking of which, when I go online, forget about it. I refuse to wait more than two seconds for a website to load. And, if I don't see exactly what I'm looking for on the home page, or if something doesn't catch my eye right away, I don't have time to drill down.
>
> Instant gratification — that rush to which our culture has become addicted — is woven into the World Wide Web. . . . But, it's not just impatience; I also don't absorb as much online as I do offline. What I see and read on the Web doesn't seem to penetrate me. In fact, sometimes I can't remember whether I simply browsed a Web site or actually ordered something, whether I

asked a question and should expect a response or I only thought about doing so.[1]

In recent years, I have become disappointed in the obvious lack of attention span exhibited by Christian teenagers. As I have spoken to teen audiences over the years, I have always believed them to be one of the toughest audiences you can find. Now it seems their attention is even harder to gain. Unless you specifically insist that all cell phones be turned off during a speaking presentation, within five minutes, many of these young people are texting their friends elsewhere or even texting other friends who are in the same room. They can't seem to pay attention to a non-electronic source for any time at all. It is rather sad and disheartening, not to mention disrespectful and rude.

When I travel, I am often invited as a guest to others' homes. It is discouraging to see many occasions when I arrive of teenagers so engrossed in a video game that they won't even look up or acknowledge a newcomer's presence when I walk in the door. If their parents make them pause the game and say hello, they will long enough to be obligatory, then it's right back to the virtual battle on the screen. It may seem extreme to many, but we have chosen to avoid owning a video game console or allowing electronic gaming in our home at all. It's not that we believe it is a sin. It's just that we feel on the scale of good, better, and best, it may not even qualify as good. So far, we have had no regrets about this decision (in 19 years of parenting).

Information Overload Resulting in Hi-Tech Stress

Dr. Robert J. Dupuis, MD, in his book *How to Avoid High Tech Stress*,[2] posits that technology is exploding at what he calls an "exponential" level. In other words, there is virtually no limit to the growth of technological development. Human beings, the ones using and trying to harness this hi-tech revolution, are limited in their ability to adapt to new ideas and concepts. He suggests that we have reached a point in history where our ability to learn, grasp, and

---

1. Ilise Benun, *Publish,* December/January 2001.
2 Robert J. Dupuis, M.D., *How to Avoid High Tech Stress* (Lafayette, LA: Huntington House, 1999).

deal effectively with technology has been surpassed by the expansive upward climb of new breakthroughs.

When we are overloaded with too much new information and we don't have enough time to process it, we get stressed out. It is a lot like being fed faster than we can chew, swallow, and digest the food. If we eat too much too fast, without giving time for our meal to settle, we get indigestion. When our brains are overloaded, without time to adapt and process the data, we get burned out and experience physical symptoms of hi-tech stress.

Another similar problem I have seen is that of adrenaline stirred by virtual stimulus but given no physical release. When we watch a movie or play a computer game that has action or terror, our body kicks in, giving us an adrenaline boost in relation to the virtual situation we find ourselves in. That is why children move around when playing video games — they are physically reacting to the threats being made to their virtual lives. The bad news is that they aren't moving enough. When watching TV, playing electronic games, or working on the computer, our bodies are stationary, and we don't have a physical release for the rush of energy we just received. In computer games and movies, our emotions are lifted and let down; we are scared senseless, then relieved. This produces physical stress and emotional frustration. I don't believe it is natural or healthy to produce adrenaline that frequently without having to exert ourselves physically to release the rush. If you don't believe me, just watch how children snap at each other when they have spent too long in front of a monitor. Or, observe how tired those of us are who spend all day in front of a computer at work. When our machine malfunctions (which happens all too frequently!), our anger immediately surfaces, and we have no physical vent for it. We have to wait until we calm down again (which will be a while, if we are forced to call tech support!). Many doctors have reported that physical exhaustion requires only physical rest for recovery. Mental exhaustion requires sleep.

Children especially can receive either information overload or emotional distress as a result of mature information that they aren't prepared to deal with. The more access children have to the media, the more likely they are to be troubled by stories they hear that, perhaps, they should not. Children often consume up to six or seven hours of digital media a day. With the privacy of hand-held devices and earphones, parents may not even know what information their children are accessing.

The Monica Lewinski scandal of the Clinton administration is an early example of a situation where hundreds of thousands of school-age children were receiving information at the same time (or before) their parents were. It used to be that parents were the channel through which children learned what was happening in the outside world. They could filter information, delay it, or exclude it altogether. That is no longer the case in most American homes.

Playing God

> Now the whole earth had one language and one speech (Gen. 11:1; NKJV).

Years ago, when technology was much more primitive, the people of the earth gathered together in a great project to establish the religion of humanism. They had determined that if they could all come together with a common language and a common currency, they could build a "global village" with a tower that would reach all the way to heaven. They could make a name for themselves and not be so scattered all over the earth. Their children could participate with them as they became a self-sufficient people. They would no longer need God because they could do anything they wanted if they could all work together for it. Even God conceded this point.

> And the LORD said, "Behold, they are one people, and they have all one language, and this is only the beginning of what they will do. And nothing that they propose to do will now be impossible for them" (Gen. 11:6).

The scientific, technological, political, and economic communities of the world have one thing in common. They exalt man and despise their Maker. They have thumbed their noses at a Holy God long enough, and I believe God is going to bring their humanistic plans to nothing. He will confuse them as He did those at the Tower of Babel over 4,000 years ago.

I'm not saying we shouldn't use technology; it can and should be used (by some) for the glory of God. God created the incredible mind of man, and many of the great advances made in science and technology have been made by godly Christians. Perhaps today's Christian youth will be the leaders in the next wave of hi-tech advances. However, most of the companies from which we buy in the tech world are heathen to the core. They hate God and promote immorality. We need to be very discerning with what we allow in our homes.

Media Fast

Many Christian leaders have recommended that, from time to time, families may need to call a complete fast from all electronic media. If the technological input in your life has been destructive to you or your family, or you see addictive tendencies arising, you may want to declare a month that is tech-free. No TV, no Internet, no digital music, no electronic games, no movies, no radio, just peace and quiet. Use the time to learn to converse with one another, read aloud as a family, play an instrument, pray, take walks outside together, or simply be quiet.

Remember, families two hundred years ago lived quite well without any electricity. Sure, life was more difficult in many ways, but it was much simpler and less hectic as well. Today, we can't even imagine living without a smartphone, something that wasn't even invented when I was growing up. In reality, our necessities for life are far fewer than we imagine. Don't get me wrong, I'm thankful for modern electronic conveniences. We own many and use them in our home. The goal, however, is for us to use them as tools to help us be more effective in doing what God has called us to do. When we are being controlled by our gadgets, we need to take back the reins. If God is leading you to "pull the plug" in your home, make sure that you use the time to draw close to Him. Turn off the voices that distract you from that "still, small voice." You may find at the end of the month that you don't care to go back!

Dads, Lead by Example!

Fathers, you must set the pace for your own household. You must lead your family by the standards you establish and live by. Your children are going to mirror you and your wife in the area of entertainment and media. You can't hold a double standard, or you will teach them to be hypocrites. If something isn't good for the children, it probably isn't good for Mom and Dad either.

The issue of technology is so big that I could write an entire book on it and still not be able to fit it all into neat little categories with all the problems instantly solved. My main goal in this chapter is to challenge you to think about the media, entertainment, technology, and the values they transmit to your family. Examine the information that is entering your home through the wires and the airwaves. Never stop considering and praying about the voices that tell you what to think about and what to believe about what you just heard. It is a lifelong process. The more involved you are with using electronic devices, the more carefully you need to evaluate their impact on your family.

'Tis a gift to be simple. 'Tis a gift to be free.[3]

---

3. Old Shaker hymn.

Chapter 4

Teaching Your Children About Purity

How can a young man keep his way pure? By guarding it according to your word (Ps. 119:9).

The advent of electronic media has allowed information to spread through every television, radio, computer, cell phone, and handheld device in America. Never have so many images and worldviews been so easily accessible with a mere click. Our culture is absolutely charged with a sexual and sensual atmosphere.

Obviously, a big part of protecting our children's innocence is by limiting and controlling the information sources. To date, we have never had cable television (after 20 years of marriage). We have Internet at our house (I work at home, so I need it for work), but we severely limit screen time with our children. As I mentioned, we always use Internet blocking and accountability software. Limiting digital media with our children is considered radical in our day and age. Young children have survived for thousands of years without electronic media, but today's families can't even conceive of life without them.

We do not expect that our family should be the standard for your family's media choices. You need to decide what is right for your own family. We do recommend, however, that less is more when it comes to electronic media.

Principles of Purity

More important than dealing with externals is the need to deal with the heart. Even Amish children sin in their hearts without all the trappings of the digital age.

Jesus said in Matthew 5:8, "Blessed are the pure in heart, for they shall see God." We want our children (and ourselves) to be pure in heart. That includes physical and sexual purity, but it goes far deeper than that. We want our children to pursue holiness, without which no one will see the Lord (see Heb. 12:14).

Holiness reflects the nature and character of God. God is holy. To be holy means we are set apart for His purposes and plans. We are unique and distinct from the sinful world around us. Our desires and pursuits are for His honor and glory. We recognize that our bodies are the temple of the Holy Spirit (1 Cor. 6:19) and that the place where He abides must be holy (1 Cor. 6:15).

In the Sermon on the Mount, Jesus put a great emphasis not on rule-keeping, but on the condition of the heart. He said that in God's sight, lust was the same as committing the act of adultery (Matt. 5:27–30). Reputation is what other people believe about you. Character is what God knows about you. Your character is who you are when you are all alone. Character is doing the right thing, even when no one will ever see or know.

1. Understanding God's Purposes for Sex

It is important for us to teach our children that God created sex. It is a wonderful gift that He intends to be enjoyed by one man and his wife in an exclusive covenant marriage (Gen. 2:24; Matt. 19:4–6). God's purposes for sex in marriage include the procreation of godly offspring (Mal. 2:14–15), the avoidance of sexual immorality because of temptation (1 Cor. 7:2), fostering loving unity and intimacy in the marriage relationship (1 Cor. 7:3–5; Heb. 13:4), and finally for pleasure (Prov. 5:18; Song of Solomon). Sex is not a dirty act, nor is it something that we should be ashamed to discuss with our children (in age-appropriate ways, of course). We need to impart to our children the truth that sex is holy, created by God, and a beautiful gift within the confines of life-long marriage between a man and his wife.

2. Purity Begins in the Heart and Mind

Our desire is that our children view their relationships with other people, on every level, as an opportunity for them to be servants and to think of others' needs rather than their own. This lack of selfishness that is cultivated in how they relate with their parents, siblings, friends, and relatives will be a good foundation for later in life when they begin to experience physical attraction toward the opposite sex. Marriage and sexuality are about serving others, not being self-centered.

I think a distinction needs to be made between physical attraction to the opposite sex, which is very natural and normal for both male and female, and lust, which God condemns. What is the difference? There is nothing ungodly about noticing physical beauty. There are a number of cases in Scripture where the Bible itself objectively notes that someone was physically beautiful or attractive (Gen. 24:16, 26:7, 29:17; 1 Sam. 16:12, 25:3; 2 Sam. 14:27; 1 Kings 1:4; Esther 1:11, 2:7; Job 42:15). This reference to beauty or attractiveness is totally free of lustful intent. It reflects the reality that God has created beauty, and He designed us to be attracted to physical beauty.

The difficulty is where we go with that attraction. If we allow ourselves to go beyond mere recognition of beauty to desiring a sexual relationship with someone who is not our spouse, then we cross the line into lust. Looking at someone (to whom we are not currently married) with a desire to have sexual relations with him or her is forbidden by Jesus. Lust is an issue of the mind and heart, and that is where Jesus places priority.

3. Avoiding a Promiscuous Attitude

In Western culture, we have been conditioned to approach relationships with a self-centered and uncommitted mindset. Most people go through multiple dating relationships before finally settling down and marrying someone, and then many go through multiple divorces or live-in relationships.

Although I was involved in dating in my early teen years, at age 15, I made a commitment not to date any young woman who was not my wife. I didn't want to waste my youth in the endless pursuit of one romantic relationship after another. My wife never dated anyone but me (and we only "dated" after we were engaged to be married, so it wasn't a trial relationship). We tell our story in a booklet and audiobook entitled *What God Has Joined Together*. We believe that going with someone and breaking up, then going with another person and breaking up, is more preparation for divorce than it is preparation for marriage.

While the purpose of this book is not to explore all of the details of how to prepare your children for marriage (we have done that in other resources we have published), we do want to encourage you to teach your children to think of saving their hearts, minds, and bodies (in terms of romantic love) for the one person they will marry.

4. Be a Safe Place for Your Children

Children are going to get their views on sexuality from somewhere. As a parent, you should be their primary source of information. Most children get their views on love, romance, and sex from books, magazines, movies, peers, TV, and music. Almost inevitably, the messages they receive from most of these sources will not be godly. Young children have no concerns whatsoever with asking their parents questions about sex. I think, though, that children can be conditioned by bad reactions on the part of their parents to stop asking.

If your children are asking questions about reproduction, where babies come from, and such, seize the moment and thank God for the opportunity to shape their worldviews in this area. If you seem uncomfortable with the topic, your children will be uncomfortable as well. Be relaxed, answer the questions that are being asked, and don't give them more information than they really need to know at their age.

For example, when a five-year-old asks, "Mommy, where did I come from?" he doesn't want a detailed description full of intimate details. He probably just wants to know that you didn't buy him at Walmart.

I would say something like, "Johnny, we were so happy when one day, five years ago, God decided to bless your mother and me with a present. God sent you to live with us."

"Yes, but how did I get here?"

"You were born. You lived for nine months in your mother's womb, and then you were born."

"What is a womb?"

"It's a special place like a little room inside of your mother's belly, where you could grow and develop."

"How did I get out?"

"God has designed the whole process in a wonderful way. When a baby is fully developed, there is a birth canal and an opening so the baby can come out of the mother's body when the baby is fully ready."

"Oh. Can I play with Legos® now?"

Most of the time, these are the kinds of discussions you have with your young children. As they get older and need more information, you may want to use anatomy charts, or better yet, let them see some animals give birth. Every child who has ever grown up on a farm has sex and reproduction all figured out before he or she turns ten. Urban and suburban life has made the teaching of sexuality far more difficult for parents.

When your children are teenagers, you may want to give them a book on reproduction that is medically accurate and supports a biblical view of sex. Try to anticipate changes that will take place in their bodies and minds and be ahead of the game. This will prepare them for what is ahead and will encourage them to trust you.

5. Finding a Mate

My goal is to develop such a close and trusting relationship with my children that when it is time for them to seek a marriage partner, they will desire to seek my counsel and blessing. I do not wish to impose my will upon them in some forceful, external way, but I do believe it is normative for parents to be involved (in prayer, in counsel, in support, in accountability, and in blessing) with their adult children during the marriage process.

If I have not been able to earn their trust and respect, then anything I try to force on them will surely backfire and be rejected. If I have been a safe place for them over the years and a reliable source of godly wisdom and counsel for them, it is my hope that they will seek out my counsel and blessing on whom they marry. I am looking forward to the day when I can help my sons find godly wives and give my daughters in marriage to godly husbands (Jer. 29:6).

6. *Faithful Christian Community*

I am firmly convinced that the Lord's desire is for us to join ourselves together in close relationship with other families who are of like heart and faith. It seems to me that, for the most part, our American churches have cultivated a very detached relational setting, where we do not really share our lives outside of the four walls of our church buildings or outside of scheduled formal meeting times. I believe it is normative for our children to find mates among those with whom they have lived, worshiped, worked, played, and ministered. God is certainly not limited to geography (my wife and I met and were married over a 1,700-mile distance); however, in general, there are often some inherent difficulties to getting to know one another when you have no sense of cultural background and no life history together.

The loss of the family culture and the greater local faith community has resulted in people opting for rather artificial and, in my view, problem-laden dating methods. Because of the lack of a potential marriage partner in their local area, many people have looked to online networking sites or similar methods to find a mate. While God certainly can, and does, bring people together through these approaches, I feel that the more ideal approach is for our children to grow up in a culture that supports their Christian values and virtues. Ideally, your family will be connected to many other like-hearted families locally with whom you share your lives.

In this type of context, the process of moving from being friends (or brothers and sisters in Christ as Paul puts it in 1 Timothy 5) to marriage partners will be far more natural and normal. The context of the family culture, and its extended folk culture, is how people were married for millennia before the advent of mass transportation, mass communication, mass media and entertainment, urbanization, government schools, feminization, and the sexualized pop culture of the twentieth century. People grew up in a family and got to know other young people in the context of families. So, when a person was interested in pursuing a marriage relationship, he or she knew the background of the person he or she wanted to marry. That person knew the other's extended family, values, personalities, and much more.

Much of what we now know about dating and romance was birthed out of the changes that occurred during modernism and the cultural revolutions that followed. We lost much that was good and acquired much that wasn't. While we cannot turn back the hands of time nor return to a different era, I believe that we can still find ways to honor Christ in our day and age and to be holy in a perverted and sensual culture.

We do not encourage our teens to date. We do not believe it is wise for them to pursue a romantic relationship with someone when they are not ready to marry. They should only pursue a relationship that may lead to marriage once they are emotionally and financially ready to marry. We believe they should then get to know one another first as friends and only pursue the possibility of an exclusive relationship once they are certain that this person has the character qualities that they would hope to find in a husband or wife.

We would encourage them to get to know the other person's family and ask a lot of questions at the outset rather than entering into a romantic relationship. Quite often, relationships can be quickly ruled out by asking some basic discovery questions. When I was interested in marriage with Brook, I contacted her father and asked if Brook was ready to be married. If he had said, "No, she has three years of college left before she wants to think about marriage," I wouldn't have attempted to pursue a relationship with her. I already knew that she loved children, wanted to have a large family (as I did), and was committed to homeschooling her future children. These were very important factors for me (among others) in deciding whom I wanted to marry. Knowing who I was and what I was looking for in a marriage (my non-negotiables) helped me to eliminate a lot of potential relationships without wasting time in months of dating.

The Bible does not ever encourage any romantic relationship outside of a covenant commitment. Only within covenant is love truly safe to grow and flourish. Covenant is the wall around the garden that allows love to have its full expression. Covenant is like a woodstove in your living room. It provides confines and context where the fires of love can burn bright and give warmth to an entire home. Inside of covenant, that romance is a wonderful, beautiful gift. Outside of covenant, romance is like a fire burning on your living room floor. It can be very dangerous. Be very cautious of encouraging your teens and young adults to pursue romantic relationships outside of a covenant commitment to marriage.

Chapter 5

The Power of Influence

At the time of this writing, my oldest son is 19. He has been working outside the home six days a week for over a year now. I'm super proud of him. He's been very responsible and is transitioning well into adulthood. The thing that became clear to me, even before he turned 18, is how little control I have over him. He has his own vehicle, his own phone, and his own life to a great extent. Because he often leaves early on Sunday morning to help lead the sound tech team at our church, my time with him is severely limited. We are both so busy that when I am home, I see him only a few hours a week. Earlier this year, our family went on the road for a couple months, and he didn't go with us. It's a whole new season for us that we are trying to figure out.

Shifting from Control to Influence

The way parenting works is that you start off parenting with 100% control. When your baby is born, he or she cannot walk, talk, feed him or herself, or even change his or her own diapers. The baby is completely dependent on you for everything. This tips the balance of power in the relationship completely to your side. As time goes on, a shift occurs whereby the parent needs to gradually and increasingly move from utilizing power (control) to using influence to help shape and direct the child. See the graphic on the following page.

I often see parents trying to parent a two-year-old with influence. They beg, cajole, plead, negotiate, bargain, and defer to a child who is making stern demands, and they end up losing the contest of wills. It's like they are afraid of their own toddler. Or, in many cases, they are trying to treat the toddler as a 21-year-old. "What cereal

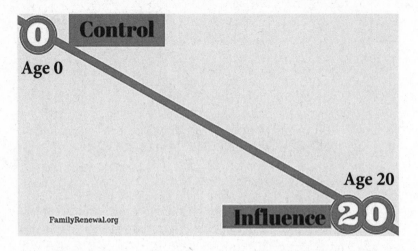

would you like to eat?" "What would you like to do today?" "Would you like to take a nap?"

If you know anything about the teaching method of "the Trivium" (see my book *Education: Does God Have an Opinion?* for more on that topic), you know that the ancient Greeks divided a child's learning into three distinct stages: Grammar, Logic, and Rhetoric. Many contemporary parents are dealing with children at a Logic (critical thinking) and Rhetoric (argument and articulation) level when they haven't even gotten to the Grammar stage (basic reading and writing). This is a wrongheaded approach.

Small children do not thrive in a world with unlimited possibilities. They need predictable boundaries. They need to know what the rules are. They need to know what they are allowed to do and what they are not. When the child is very young, the parent needs to be the unquestioned authority figure. As the child grows and develops, the momentum shifts away from that role to one of being a coach, advisor, mentor, cheerleader, friend, and trusted confidant.

For the most part, I don't tell "19" what to do. I ask questions to help guide him through his decisions. I want him to learn how to think and make decisions. I don't want to make those choices for him. I help him identify his goals and develop strategies for meeting them.

My two-year-old, on the other hand, does what I tell her.

She doesn't get a vote. Now don't get me wrong. There are massive amounts of love, tenderness, affection, fun, enjoyment, and delight that is the context that surrounds our relationship. I'm not an unfeeling dictator. But when I tell "two" she isn't allowed to go outside without permission, I mean it. It isn't up to negotiation.

The problem that I see is that parents invert the chart. They try to raise their toddlers with influence and their teens with control. That is a recipe for disaster!

Purchase and Save Influence

The only way to avoid this trap is to buy influence with your children during their growing years. I think of influence as a commodity that you can purchase or give away. I have a "relationship savings bank" with my children where I invest "influence dollars" that I may need to withdraw someday in the future.

> The kingdom of heaven is like treasure hidden in a field, which a man found and covered up. Then in his joy he goes and sells all that he has and buys that field. Again, the kingdom of heaven is like a merchant in search of fine pearls, who, on finding one pearl of great value, went and sold all that he had and bought it (Matt. 13:44–46).

As parents, what could be more important than gaining influence in the life of our child? What would we be willing to sell in order to buy it? Seriously. Would we give up a car for it? A larger house? A big screen TV? The fact is, it may cost all those things and more.

> For whoever would save his life will lose it, but whoever loses his life for my sake will find it. For what will it profit a man if he gains the whole world and forfeits his soul? Or what shall a man give in return for his soul? (Matt. 16:25–26).

What will it be worth if our children grow up to have a good career and great financial success, but don't know the Lord? If our priorities are toward worldly gain rather than sacrifice for Christ's Kingdom, why do we think our children will have a different goal than us?

Buying Influence

How does a parent obtain influence capital? There are two primary forces in influence: time and affirmation.

Time

The most important ingredient in obtaining influence in the life of your child is quantity time. If you want to influence another person, you need to have access to them. If you have never met me, never heard of me, and have never heard or read any of my ideas, I will have no influence in your life. I need to have access to you in order to have influence. It is slightly reductionistic, but I could almost say that whoever spends the most time with your child wins.

What is sad and shocking about this is that most Christian parents give away this important force for influence with almost no regard whatsoever. When we consider the statistics we talked about earlier, of 70% of all churched youth leaving the church before their high school graduation and most saying they want nothing to do with Christianity, something has broken down. Somehow, Christian parents have lost their influence. Their children no longer respect them and their beliefs and values. Someone somewhere else has become the most important, influential person in that child's life.

It has been said that a child's sense of self-worth is determined by what the most important person in his or her life thinks of him or her. If that person is the parent, the child will do what he or she needs to do in order to maintain the approval of the parents. We all crave acceptance. We want to fit in. But when a child's allegiance has shifted away from the parents to someone or something else, the parents can no longer direct and shape as they once did. So, who has taken hold of the child's heart and mind? Who has captured and lured him or her away from the parents? I think we can answer this question by asking, "Who has access to our child, and who is spending the most time with him or her?"

When seeking to solve a crime, Sherlock Holmes would always ask two questions: "Who had the motive, and who had the ability?" For someone to sway the child away from the parent, that person needed to have access to the child.

According to the Bureau of Labor Statistics (2018), the average adult male spends over 5 hours per day in entertainment and recreation. The average woman, ages 35–44, spends almost four hours per day in leisure and electronic media. She spends 1.61 hours helping and interacting with household members. For American adults, sleep is the biggest chunk of their time, followed by entertainment and sports and then employed work. Only 14% of American adults factor in religious or civic activities as part of their normal routine. The average amount of time parents (combined) spend helping their children under age 6 is about two hours per day. The average time they spend taking care of children ages 6–12 is only about an hour per day.[1]

Men spend only 26 minutes a day giving care to their own children.[2] So the best-case scenario for working parents is spending only one to two hours a day interacting with their children (this includes feeding them, bathing them, getting them dressed, having a conversation with them, etc.).

When you consider that a child lives 24 hours each day, for 22–23 hours each day, they are being occupied by some other agency than their parents (and 23 hours and 34 minutes without direction from Dad!). If this is you, who is buying up the rest of your child's time (life)?

School

According to the National Center for Education & the Economy, the average American student spends 180 days in school each year, and each school day is 6.8 hours per day (of classroom instruction).[3] This adds up to 1,224 hours of seat instruction every year. From K–12, that adds up to 15,912 hours of instruction before the child turns 18. That is a lot of influence!

So, schools obviously own a major chunk of a child's day. If you factor transportation, a student easily spends 7.5 hours a day at school (not counting extra-curricular activities). This is a mas-

---

1. https://www.bls.gov/charts/american-time-use/activity-by-age.htm.
2. https://www.bls.gov/news.release/atus.nr0.htm.
3. http://ncee.org/2018/02/statistic-of-the-month-how-much-time-do-students-spend-in-school/.

sive force for influence because parents send their children to these schools and tell their children to "learn." They go as sponges, ready to soak up and receive whatever instruction is given to them (even it if conflicts with a biblical worldview).

I often say, in terms of school influence, that there are three teachers in every school. There is the person who stands up front and says, "I am your teacher." There is the curriculum, which is a teacher. And then there is the force that ends up actually influencing the child more than any other: their peers.

Multimedia

According to Pew Research in 2018, 95% of teens have access to smartphones, and 45% say they are online "almost constantly."[4] Pew Research says, according to their analysis of the Bureau of Labor Statistics' data, teens today spend about an hour a day after school doing homework and between 5–6 hours in leisure. Most of that time is spent engaging in digital media (screen time).[5] It is clear that you can account for 14 to 15 hours of their awake hours each day divided between school, peers, and media influence. That just doesn't leave a lot of time for Mom and Dad.

The Barna Group conducted research in 2016 commissioned by the American Bible Society and found that only 3% of American teens read the Bible on a daily basis,[6] but nearly ¾ of all teens say they check their smartphone for messages in the morning before they do anything else.[7] This generation's teens are being influenced by electronic media and peers, not the Bible and their parents. When you consider that the media palette for Christian youth is almost indistinguishable from that of their non-Christian friends, it becomes obvious that video games, popular secular music, and

4. https://www.pewinternet.org/2018/05/31/teens-social-media-technology-2018/.
5. https://www.pewresearch.org/fact-tank/2019/02/20/the-way-u-s-teens-spend-their-time-is-changing-but-differences-between-boys-and-girls-persist/.
6. 2016 Teen State of the Bible: http://news.americanbible.org/blog/entry/corporate-blog/over-scheduled-teens-struggle-to-find-time-for-the-bible.
7. https://www.pewresearch.org/fact-tank/2019/08/23/most-u-s-teens-who-use-cellphones-do-it-to-pass-time-connect-with-others-learn-new-things/.

Hollywood are saturating the minds of today's churched youth. The instruction they receive in government school is not religiously neutral; it is anti-Christian. The media they consume on their smartphones is largely antagonistic to the Christian faith.

Church: The Parents' Silver Bullet

Parents have not only "delegated" or "outsourced" (the more accurate word is "abdicated") the training of their own children to people (in most cases) they barely even know, but they have done so to those who are hostile to their own faith, values, and political beliefs. Why would anyone do that?

Rather than taking responsibility for the spiritual teaching and discipleship of their own children, they have assumed that a "religiously neutral" government can teach their child academics, and the Sunday school, junior church, and/or youth group will provide the spiritual instruction their children need. This thinking couldn't be more dangerous or wrongheaded. While there are definite exceptions (and I truly hope your church is as different as you think it is!), most children's church curriculum is shallow and consists mainly of having young children color pictures of Noah's Ark and make fun crafts with popsicle sticks (I used to work in children's ministry, so I have some experience with this). Our goal in children's ministry (which was often just a babysitting service so parents didn't have to teach their children to sit still for the regular church service) was to keep your child alive for an hour until you returned. If they sang a few songs, heard a few Bible verses, ate cookies, drank punch, and didn't need to go to the emergency room, we considered it a great success!

Again, some programs are better than this, but in my experience, that is pretty average. A woman came up to me after hearing me speak at a parenting seminar and shared her observation. She told me that she was the children's ministry director at a megachurch that had over 1,000 children and youth. She said that in 20 years serving as the director, she had never had one parent ask to the see the Sunday school curriculum they used. She lamented that they could be teaching children every Sunday that "Satan is Lord," and in her words, "Most parents would never know, unless the child brought it up. Most parents just see a sign that says, 'Drop your children off here and run!' They don't know us, don't know our names, and most don't even check to see if we have done background checks for the ministry workers [which they thankfully do!]. They just trust us. We're a church, so they trust us. And they shouldn't. We do the best we can to teach their children something substantial, but they don't know that we do. They just assume it."

I learned so much bad theology in children's church and Sunday school that I am still trying to unravel myself from it all. In the 1990s, I can't tell you how many churches I knew of that would just insert an animated VeggieTales® video to entertain the children until "class was over." I can assure you, 30 minutes of VeggieTales® a week as a child and a lot of pizza parties and Christian rock concerts as a teen in youth group is not going to equip your child to stand against the onslaught of anti-Christian propaganda he or she will get slammed with in a freshman psychology, sociology, or philosophy class at a state or secular university.

Please, don't misunderstand me. I'm not against the church doing everything it can to help aid in the process of discipling and spiritually mentoring children and youth. Anything they do is a wonderful supplement. But it is not their job to raise your child. Your children belong to you, and if the job of teaching them Bible doctrine, theology, and Christian apologetics/biblical worldview is going to happen, you are going to have to take full and complete responsibility for it.

Affirmation

I wrote an entire chapter called "The Power of Affirmation" for our book *Pitchin' A Fit! Overcoming Angry & Stressed-Out Parenting,* so I won't duplicate efforts here. But for your consideration, if you buy back time, which gives you potential for influence (and I hope you buy every minute and second you can!), you need to ensure that you make the most of that time. It does no good to keep your children home to protect them from harmful outside influences but then make home a miserable place they hate.

Your children need to know, and feel, that they are deeply loved (and liked!) by you. You need to make sure they know that you are *for them*. Sometimes children feel the decisions we make are for *our* benefit. They need to know that we want the best for *them*. We are on *their* side. *We* are their biggest allies and cheerleaders. You should seek to spend more time with them than anyone else and affirm them more than anyone else in their lives. If you do that, you will buy influence. If your children like you and respect you and value your opinion, they will come to you later in life, seeking direction and counsel for major life decisions (like what college to attend, what career to pursue, whom to marry, etc.). If you have not established that trust and open communication when they are young, it will not go well for you to try to force them to comply with your desires when they are older teens and young adults. Force and coercion do not go well as motivators for teens who are physically larger than you! You need to learn how to transition from authority figure to role model and life coach.

Have a Goal

You need to know why you are parenting. Thirty years from now, what will define success for you as a parent? How will you know if you have accomplished your goals if they aren't clear in your own mind? Do you know why you are raising your children? Is it simply so they can get good grades, go to college, have careers, pay the bills, retire, move to Florida, spend their children's inheritance, and die?

What kind of persons do you hope your children will become? How do you hope they will teach and train your grandchildren?

Develop a Family Mission Statement

In our living room hangs a large poster I designed and had printed. It reads, "We exist to know, love and serve God, and to love and serve others." It is our "family mission statement." It is the "true north" on our life compass. It reminds us of why we were created and what we are here for. It helps calibrate every decision we make. Does an opportunity or activity match up with our stated life goal? If it does not, we don't do it. I would encourage you to develop a family mission statement of your own so you and your children have a clear vision of why you are here on this earth and what you need to be aiming toward each day.

A Multi-Generational Vision

Personally, I think the true success of my parenting will be evidenced in the lives of my great-grandchildren. If my children's children are discipling their children well, then I will feel like a success.

> Tell your children of it, and let your children tell their children, and their children to another generation (Joel 1:3).

Chapter 6

Apologetics Begins at Home

The great thing about being available for your children and teenagers is that you can be the go-to person for their questions. You have the privilege to lead them to the Lord through His Word. This isn't always easy, though!

I vividly remember receiving a letter on my pillow from my 13-year-old daughter. It was full of questions she wanted me to help her understand. Much of my life is dedicated to teaching and equipping the Body of Christ to study and defend God's Word. However, I am reminded that my first and primary mission field is always my own family.

Here is a list of some of the questions that were going through my daughter's mind:

> Why did God make emotions?
> What did God do before He made everything?
> Would the world be any different if I had never been born?
> How old is the earth?
> When were angels made?
> If Mary is Jesus' mother, was she God's wife?
> Do I have to be baptized to be a Christian?
> Did all the people before Jesus go to hell?
> How is God a king and servant at the same time?
> What does God look like?
> Did God marry Adam and Eve?
> Do people sin after they become Christians?

> How does God want me to treat people I don't
> understand?
> What does "carnal" mean?
> How do I become holy, pure, and perfect? (Things
> the Bible commands.)
> What does it mean to hide God's Word in my heart?
> What will I do in heaven?
> How can I help all the people in the whole world?
> God is love. If I love someone, is it God's love?
> > People hate God, but they also love too. How?
> What does "circumcise your heart" mean?
> How are we "in the world, but not of it"?
> Do babies go to heaven when they die?
> How can God be Grace and Justice at the same
> time? Aren't they opposites?
> How does God love and hate at the same time?
> (Aren't they opposites?)
> What are angels like?
> Why did God make life?

These are serious and important questions. You will either answer these questions adequately for your children, or they will make their decisions about them from other sources. Nothing is more important in your list of things to do than teaching your own children the truth.

> Do your best to present yourself to God as one
> approved, a worker who has no need to be ashamed,
> rightly handling the word of truth (2 Tim. 2:15).

If you don't know the answer to these and similar questions, I encourage you to study and learn so that you can teach your children. You can only teach what you yourself know. There are a lot of great apologetics resources and curriculum programs available for people of all ages and study levels. My website[1] is a great place to start finding good information.

---

1. ChristianWorldview.net

Be A Safe Place for Your Children/Teens

Teens need to know they can talk to you about anything and that you are a safe place for them. If they have questions, concerns, fears, doubts, disagreements, etc., they need to know that you will listen. If you shut them down with confrontation and anger, they won't talk to you. Parents often overreact when their teenagers push back on their beliefs. That is just natural and normal. If your teen tells you he or she isn't sure if he or she is a Christian, doesn't know if God exists, doesn't know why you can't have sex before marriage, thinks he or she might be gay, or whatever, you need to purpose ahead of time not to overreact. Teens will go through phases, hormones, and seasons of depression and doubt. For the most part, these are all fairly common rites of passage.

I'm thankful that so far, we haven't had a lot of extreme reactions or emotions from our teens, but I've determined that we will do our best to love them and remain calm regardless of what they may throw at us. If you don't know the answer to a tough question, admit it, and be willing to search the answer out with them. Be willing to learn together. Sometimes teens just want to test the waters. They want to see what will happen if they drop a bombshell on you. They want to know if you will still love and accept them. Obviously, we can't embrace and affirm sinful behavior, but don't assume a bad day will define your child's life.

Being available for your teens also means being ready to talk whenever they are, which is usually not convenient for you. I have a daughter whose mind goes into gear at 11:00 p.m. That's not my ideal time to have theological discussions! But I'll take them when I can get them because I may not get another opportunity. If you are too busy for your children and teens when they want to talk, they will be too busy for you when you want to talk to them in the future.

Chapter 7

The Seven-Year Teaching Method

Then Moses commanded them: "At the end of every seven years . . . you shall read this law before them in their hearing. Assemble the people — men, women, and children . . . so they can listen and learn to fear the LORD your God and follow carefully all the words of this law. Their children, who do not know this law, must hear it and learn to fear the LORD your God . . ." (Deut. 31:10–13; NIV).

Not long ago I was talking with a friend of mine who is a Christian parent of 11 children. To maintain a close relationship with his children, he often takes a child with him when he makes deliveries for his business. He told me about an experience he recently had with his seven-year-old daughter.

They had to wait a few minutes in the truck before unloading, so he grabbed his pocket Bible and began to read to his daughter. Shortly after he began reading, he became aware that his daughter was not familiar with the story. This surprised my friend, who was certain that he would have told his daughter this well-known account in Scripture. His older children knew the story, and he reads the Bible regularly to all his children, so how could his seven-year-old have missed this?

He was reminded of the Scripture in Deuteronomy 31 in which God instructed all His people, from oldest to youngest, to review

His entire law every seventh year. Why do you suppose God gathered all the people together every seven years and had them listen to the same words again?

My Own Experience

As I contemplated this passage, I reflected on my own life. When I was seven, I knew all the major Bible stories and wanted people to know that I was a Christian. I was the Bible quizzing champ at our Sunday school and won prizes for memorization at Vacation Bible School. I believed the Bible to be true and wanted to obey God.

Seven years later, at age 14, I was faced with an entirely different set of circumstances. I was dealing with peer pressure; struggling with dating issues; transitioning into manhood; wrestling with being submitted to authority; learning about conformity, popularity, and fitting in; etc. My relationship with God was at a real turning point.

At 21, my world changed again. As a single young man, I was in the middle of national ministry, waiting on God to bring me a wife in His timing, and past the turmoil of the teen years. God had been merciful to me in allowing me to be discipled by loving brothers and sisters who helped to demonstrate a godly lifestyle for me and to shape my worldview. I was at rest, enjoying life, and serving the Lord.

At 28, I was happily married, a father of three sweet children, and I had learned a lot about myself. I was trying to balance the demands of work and ministry with investing properly in my wife and children. I was learning how to put into practice all the things I had been taught as a child about life and family.

When I was 7, I wanted to avoid getting into trouble; when I was 14, I wanted to fit in; when I was 21, I wanted direction for my life; and at 28 . . . I wanted a nap.

Teaching Our Children

I have observed that Christian parents often do a decent job of training their first child or two, but they often slack off with their later ones. I guess they get tired. Or perhaps they assume they have already taught their children all the important lessons of life.

However, it was, in fact, the older ones, not the younger ones, who received that focused instruction.

God has, in His infinite wisdom, given us everything we need that pertains to life and godliness (2 Pet. 1:3). Our Lord was good to include in His Word this nugget of wisdom for us to discover. We need to come back to the fundamental principles of life at least once every seven years. As each season of life develops, we find that the unchanging truth of God's Word confronts us in a new and unexpected way. This is a great concept for us as parents, or for those in teaching ministry to the Church, to grasp. We need periodic review, and the younger generation needs to hear some truths for the first time.

I have attempted to lead my children through the entire Bible, verse-by-verse, on a seven-year cycle. I would like for them to hear the entire Bible read three times before they leave my home. Of course, I want them to develop their own disciplines of reading the Bible themselves, but I want to help set that example by reading it to them (as much as possible) daily.

I would encourage you as parents to cycle back through the Scriptures to make sure you cover the same content several times with your children as they go through the various stages of development.

Chapter 8

How I Taught My Children to Sit Still and Be Quiet

"Be still, and know that I am God" (Ps. 46:10a).

When my wife and I were first married, we invited a family to our house for a visit. They had seven children, ages 1 to 14, who were all homeschooled. We sat together in our living room for three hours, enjoying fellowship and conversation. I was amazed by their children for several reasons.

First, they sat quietly, for three hours, without getting up and running around! I had never seen children do this. At first, I would have suspected that perhaps this was abnormal and unhealthy — something that shouldn't be encouraged — until I realized that they were all enjoying listening to the conversation!

The second thing that surprised me was that they did not interrupt the adult conversation but were content to listen rather than talk and share their own thoughts and ideas. Again, I would have thought that perhaps they were just socially inept and that they didn't know how to communicate, until their parents would ask them to share something or my wife and I asked them a question. Then they would smile and speak up in a clear and appropriately loud voice to answer our question. Sometimes they would ask us a question in return. They were truly interested in other people.

Even though I did not yet have children, I knew that I must learn the secret of how one family could raise a houseful of well-mannered, respectful, appropriately quiet, and pleasantly conversant children. To this day, I have not met a family that lives in such peace and harmony with each other and those outside their family. So, I asked them how they did it. Their answer was not at all what I would have suspected. While some people would consider their decisions to be extreme, I could not deny that they had extremely positive results from their methods. They were not at all harsh or legalist but rather had a very loving and kind demeanor as they all interacted together as a family.

Positive Socialization

Their first secret, they informed me (rather tongue-in-cheek), was to keep their children away from other children! This seemed so contrary to all the parenting advice given by "experts" in books and articles. They said their children were not permitted to spend time alone with other children their own age but that their family always tried to interact with other families as a family unit rather than as individuals. They did have interaction with other children, but it was always in a supervised context with their parents present to provide careful oversight.

The Bible often warns against harmful peer influences and insists upon the superior benefits of having children influenced by those who are older and wiser (see Prov. 13:20 and 1 Cor. 15:33).

(I write extensively on the topic of "socialization" in my books *Education: Does God Have an Opinion?* and *Answers for Homeschooling.*)

The Simple Life

Secondly, they did not watch television or play video games. They did not listen to aggressive music or waste time being foolish, so they had lots of time to do real work with their hands (planting a garden, carrying firewood, etc.) or read a book together as a family. They lived a very simple life in a simple house, with very little clutter. I once asked them how they could fit nine people so comfortably into such a small house, and they answered that they didn't want a larger house because then they would just accumulate more stuff. They wanted life to be basic and simple. That is so unlike most families.

Proper Nutrition

Third, they completely eliminated sugar and caffeine from their diet. This made a lot of sense to me. It is completely unfair to give children substances that pump them up and make them hyper and then expect them to sit still and be quiet. Make it easier for them and yourself by giving them a good wholesome diet. We don't completely avoid sugar in our home, but we seek to reduce food options that ramp up hyperactive behavior and/or reduce immunity and overall health.

Daily Family Worship

Fourth, they had a time of family worship every morning before the father went to work (he has a workshop on his own property, so if the children need attention or direction during the day, he is available). They explained they would read the Word of God and have a time of singing and prayer every morning. Every child was present and was expected to be still. All the children who were old enough would sit on a chair or couch, and the baby would be held by the mother. They would begin this process from birth, so the children never thought it was strange. They would also read books together as a family at night, so they had even more practice sitting still and listening.

An Incremental Process

As you might expect, my wife and I began to implement many of these principles (some to a lesser degree) with our own children as they came along. I doubt that we have followed these basic principles as thoroughly as our friends (especially eliminating clutter!), but we have seen very good fruit from many of these practices. The goal is not to create a legalist set of rules, and one family's approach will not automatically work well for another family, but there are some general guiding principles they implemented that make sense to me.

Family Worship Time

For families who have not done daily devotions (family worship time) with their children from birth, I would suggest that you ease into the process. Start with 5 minutes a day. Then work up to 10 and then 15. Eventually, most children will easily sit still for an hour or more. You can read the Bible for 5 minutes, sing for 10 (this is something in which they are participating, so they are less likely to get bored), and then have a short time of prayer. Our family usually meets from half an hour to an hour every morning. We try to read a chapter from the Bible each day. (Of course, we also discuss in depth what we are reading, so sometimes our progress is a bit slow.) A certain amount of predictability and structure is required so the children know what to expect, but parents can feel a great liberty to do what they feel is best for each morning meeting. Your family doesn't need to look like any other family, and your version of "Bible time" may be completely different than ours or anyone else's. That's great. Just try to be consistent about reading the Bible; praying; and singing psalms, hymns, and spiritual songs (Eph. 5:19) together as a family.

Start Young

There is usually a bit of resistance that is expressed once a child reaches the toddler years. Once a baby can crawl, he or she would rather be on the floor moving around than sitting on Mama's lap. There will be plenty of time for that during the day but not during "Bible time." This is a time to sit still and be quiet. Not only does this teach the child self-control and good listening habits, but most importantly, it gives him or her a necessary foundation of knowing and understanding the Word of God.

For a child who is around one year old, Brook simply holds the child on her lap and gently restrains him or her when he or she wants to get down. The child will probably cry and fuss at first, which makes it hard for the other children to hear the Bible lesson, but that is okay. Remember that training, rather than merely getting through a lesson, is one of the primary objectives here. When the child gets a bit older, say 1½ to 4 years old, he or she will probably give you some resistance to sitting still and being quiet. This is where parenting comes in. You can set the lesson aside for a moment and focus on teaching your child obedience. You won't win this battle in a day, or even in a month. You will win it by doing it every day, day after day, week after week for years.

We have found that by the time a child is 3 or 4 years old (assuming there are no developmental delays in the child), if we have been consistent, he or she usually begins to embrace this time without much of a struggle. As our children get older and approach the teen years, they can begin to contribute very meaningfully by sharing with the rest of the family the things the Lord is teaching them from the family lesson or their own personal Bible study time.

A Day in Our Life

We've had days where it seemed that all we did was train our children, and we couldn't even finish reading the selected Bible passage. That is okay. We don't get upset about it. We are meeting our goals and objectives. Our children are learning to sit still, listen, and be obedient. The purpose of sitting still and listening is to give your children the tools they need (self-discipline) to be able to learn and be successful in life.

During our Bible time, we want our children to ask questions if there is anything they don't understand. It is designed to be interactive. I try to draw out each child by asking questions so they can demonstrate understanding of what we have studied. Usually by age 5 or so, we see remarkable progress in our children's abilities to be still and listen to adult conversations.

We have a personal preference to have our children with us during church meetings rather than sending them to age-segregated Sunday schools or "Junior Church." Most families cannot have their children sit with them during the entire service, even if they wanted to, because the children will not be quiet and obedient that long. The key for us has been to practice this every day at home. Our children sit through the equivalent of a sermon each morning, so doing so again on Sunday at church is no big deal for them.

For me, Bible time works best in the morning before work. For some families, it works best at night, after dinner (or some other time of the day). There isn't a right or wrong to this; the main thing is to make sure you are consistent. We like to read books in the evenings or sometimes watch an educational video or Christian film at night as a family. Whatever works for your family is great; use the time to instill the right kind of values into your children and teach them self-control.

What about Toys? (Brook)

When Israel and I share about how beneficial that simple Bible time has been for our family, one of the first questions we are asked is "What about toys?" When we first began our journey as a family trying to teach our young crew how to sit quietly during church services, I took along little items to help distract our children about eight years old and younger (little fidget toys, coloring books, etc.). I found that all I really gained out of that whole process was trying to manage a side-circus! I'd whisper to the little buddy with the crayons not to whistle while he colored, and I'd counsel my little girl not to grab and fight over her favorite book with her little brother . . . it was a mess! So, we started "going solo." We didn't use any toys or books during our family Bible time!

Now, I know that sounds extreme, and it took a few weeks for the expectations to adjust, but after that, we were truly amazed at the focus little children could give! Our littles started to tell us phrases they had heard during our Bible time or in a sermon. They laughed at funny illustrations, and I'm sure there was a whole lot that went over their heads. I'm okay with that. We provide lots of time during the rest of our day with age-appropriate lessons and bring the biblical accounts to a more reachable understanding through pictures, but what my young children gained was a visual awareness that church isn't just for children. They will spend, Lord willing, many more years as adults than children. It is really important to me that the training we're giving them gives them a vision for godliness during their adult years.

What started out as an exercise in faith that our children would eventually gain something out of those sessions of listening to the Bible being read every morning has borne fruit. We've seen our children, usually around ages 8–10, begin to catch more and more out of Bible time, willing to listen to full sermons. It's a valuable fruit worth the cultivation effort.

In the end, the goal is to help our children focus their attention on the wonder and depth of God's Word. We do this by showing them how to calm their bodies for a short time as we lead them again and again to the Living Water.

Dad Should Lead (Israel)

This daily training is something that is ideally the father's responsibility, and he should be leading this effort. Men, it is not primarily your wife's job to train your children; it is your job. She is your helpmeet, not the other way around. You need to take the time to invest in your children.

> Fathers, do not provoke your children to anger, but bring them up in the discipline and instruction of the Lord (Eph. 6:4).

The reason men should (ideally) lead family Bible time is for them as much as it is the children. You learn best by teaching, and fathers need to be transformed by the Word along with their families. I see so many families where Mom is the spiritual leader, and Dad just watches movies and sports. This sends a message to the children that Dad doesn't think all this Bible stuff is important. I talk more about the importance of Dad leading in spiritual teaching in my book *Answers for Homeschooling: Top 25 Questions Critics Ask*.

As an aside, I think it is important to note that I own my own business, and at this season in my life, I work from home. So, daily family worship is easier for us than it will be for some. However, I have also worked a regular work schedule outside the home, and we made it work then as well. If you can't find the consistency to meet together every day with Dad, maybe Mom can lead daily Bible time and Dad can join once or twice a week (maybe weekends). The goal is not to be legalistic about anything, but it is to prioritize the Word of God together as a family.

When Dad Can't or Won't Lead

For a wife who has a husband who is unable to lead his family in daily Scripture study and worship (perhaps because of a unique work requirement where he is gone for days on end, he is unsaved, or he is just unwilling), much of this training can be done by the wife. It is never ideal to have only one parent involved in this daily training. I know that neither my wife nor I could do it very well alone, but if necessary, we each would do it individually. It is of primary importance to us. A single parent can lead family worship alone if they have no spouse to help.

I would advise a wife to share this chapter with her believing husband and ask him to lead the family in daily family worship. If he will not, then do not nag your husband. You, as the sanctifying spouse, can be an agent of grace to your children. When your husband is gone, gather your children for singing, Bible reading, and prayer. Don't make it an event that everyone hates. Keep it moving and keep the lessons short, especially at first. If you don't know what you are doing, that's okay; most of the rest of us don't either. If you have never had family worship modeled for you, that's okay; almost no one has. The good news is, your children will have it modeled for them, and it will be much easier for them when it is their turn to become parents.

Encourage Your Children to Have Their Own Prayer and Bible Time

It is also important to encourage your children and teens to have a habit of Bible study on their own each day. I was talking with a friend who served in the military as a young man. When he left home, he found himself in a far more ungodly environment than the conservative Christian home in which he had been raised. It was his already established practice of daily prayer and Bible reading that helped anchor him and keep him on track in the face of new temptations.

Another dad told me that when his son went to the military, it was the discipline of daily prayer that kept him on course spiritually. This father said, "We taught our children to pray about everything. We didn't just pray at meals or bedtime. As events unfolded during the day, we would turn to the Lord in prayer and speak to God in prayer as naturally as we would speak to each other." Habits linger. If we help form the right habits early, they tend to remain.

In recent years, having our children do Bible quizzing through a local quiz district in which our church participates has been amazing! My older teens in the past three years have memorized the entire books of John, 1 and 2 Peter, 1 and 2 Corinthians, and Hebrews . . . word for word! The camaraderie of learning and practicing with their team makes it fun and competitive. Most importantly, they are getting God's Word inside of them, and we know it never returns void (see Isa. 55:11)! Scripture memory is so important for them as they grow and mature.

A Time and Place for Everything

It is not always important for children to sit still and be quiet. They are children and should be allowed to run around, play, have fun, and be noisy. We don't want them to be miserable during their whole childhood. But they do need to learn how to quiet down and behave appropriately in certain situations. You don't want them acting up at a funeral, a wedding, a church service, or when guests come over for dinner. There is a time and place for being rowdy, and there is a time to be silent and respectful. Loving our neighbor requires that we put the needs of others above ourselves. There is a time for every activity under heaven (see Eccles. 3:1). Once they have mastered the ability to control their bodies to be appropriately quiet and still, they will eventually learn to appreciate, and even enjoy, the ability to do so when necessary.

Learning Social Skills

Regarding positive social interaction with adults and other children, your children will need practice. My wife works with our children to practice shaking someone's hand, looking them in the eye, speaking up in an appropriately loud and clear voice, and being genuinely interested in other people instead of just themselves. We have some strong introverts in our home, and we still have a long way to go in these areas, but we are seeing slow progress. Using church and other social activities is a great way for them to put into practice the skills they are rehearsing at home.

A Long Obedience in the Same Direction

As I always tell my wife, "Parenting is a marathon, not a sprint. We win by being consistent day after day for years." Then I facetiously add, "Parenting is very, very easy. We just need to do all of the right things every day from the time that our child is born until he or she turns 20, and everything will turn out great!" Those last two lines always get a look from my wife that says, "That doesn't sound easy to me!" The fact is, it isn't easy. There are lots of trials and errors, failures and successes, but in the long run, you do see good fruit from a "long obedience in the same direction." This is not to mean that if you do all the right things, your child will never sin or make bad choices, but it is generally true that a child will most often continue in the trajectory to which he or she has become inclined.

Parenting Is a Marathon, Not a Sprint

Don't expect short-term gains. This is a long-term project. You may not notice much improvement in your children for weeks or months or maybe even a couple of years. That's okay. Just keep being faithful. God will reward your diligence over time. This is not about legalistically obeying rules, but rather about passing on your heart and love for the Lord to your children. They will usually rise to meet your own love and worship of the Savior. You are leading, they are following. Make sure that your own heart is clean and pure before the Lord and that you are not simply following a rigid duty but are always motivated from a heart of love. This is not about trying to look good on the outside, but on having the right desires and motives. May the Lord grant you wisdom and grace as you pursue these changes.

Chapter 9

Heart Check for Parents

Train up a child in the way he should go; even when
he is old he will not depart from it (Prov. 22:6).

A young child's worldview is very complicated. While a child is
born with inclinations, he or she is not born with understanding.
To know and comprehend something, you must first have some
experience with which to compare and evaluate. An infant has no
idea what is normal in the world. For instance, if you were driving
down the road and noticed a neon-pink sheep grazing in a pasture,
you would certainly stop your car and take a photo. Sheep are not
supposed to be pink! When a one-year-old sees the same sheep, the
infant doesn't know that he or she should be amazed. From the
child's limited base of experience, he or she reasons that perhaps
most sheep are pink. The scene is not odd to him or her.

What a sacred trust we have as parents! Our God-given responsibility is to teach our child, from his or her first breath, what is
normal and what is right or correct. May our Lord be merciful to
us and help us to never lead our children into falsehood and error.

Is Normal Just a Setting on the Dryer?

In our age of relativism (the view that there is no absolute moral
truth), it seems too absolutist to insist that there can be such a
standard as "normal." "After all," the skeptic may muse, "what is
normal for you may not be normal for me." The word "normal"
comes from the Latin *normalis*, which means "According to a square
or rule" (Webster's 1828). Anyone who has ever tried to build a

house knows that you can't do it unless you adhere to absolute principles. You must have some universal standard of measure. Plumb, square, and level must mean the same things to everyone on the work crew. If you don't all use the same rules of measurement, you will end up with disaster. You only recognize crooked if you know what is straight.

So it is in our day of pop-culture parenting. Many children today grow up being planted in soil that is abnormal (irregular, deformed). Some parents have a crooked worldview and distorted ideas of what it means to raise children. Many received their notions from the postmodern smorgasbord of pop-psychology parenting blogs, daytime talk shows, self-proclaimed family experts, or maybe just from bad experiences they carried over from their own childhood. Whether they are too loose in their parenting approach or too tight, they are unbalanced in their approach to raising their children, and their children suffer because of it. The beliefs and actions of most parents are totally arbitrary, unpredictable, and driven by mood swings rather than a biblical theology of parenthood.

There is a difference between what is common and what is normal. Normal should be defined by the nature of God as described in His Word. Common is how the majority of people in a certain society choose to live. The majority are often wrong and dysfunctional. Look at how many Germans supported Adolph Hitler! Even if everyone agrees with concentration camps, they will never reflect "normal" behavior but rather abnormal and deviant. We desire to be normal but not common.

Who Is in Charge?

The Bible teaches that children do not belong to parents, at least not ultimately. Some believe that "It takes a village to raise a family." They feel that parental rights do not exist and everyone is responsible for everyone else's children. People with the "village" mentality would agree with the statement that children do not belong to their parents, but their view may lead them to meddle in the lives of others and impose themselves in situations where their involvement is neither desired nor appropriate. The Bible, however, teaches something very different than this vogue concept of the communal ownership of children.

> Behold, children are a heritage from the LORD, the fruit of the womb a reward (Ps. 127:3).

In Ezekiel 16:20–21, God emphatically declares ownership of the offspring of His people. He proclaims that these children were born to Him. God, in His infinite wisdom and mercy, has chosen some of us to be stewards and caretakers of His children.

Inappropriate Correction

The mistreatment of children by their parents is one of the most reprehensible ideas of which we can conceive. There is, as Karl Marx mockingly said in *The Communist Manifesto*, "The most hallowed of relations" between a parent and child. There is a natural bond that is divinely infused between an excited new parent and the helpless child he or she holds. Yet, despite this natural and normal connection of heart and soul, there are those who, for whatever reason, neglect that holy trust and wound the body and emotions of the child within their care.

Appropriate discipline of a child is normal. The authority of the parent is normal. C.S. Lewis in *Mere Christianity* says, "[B]adness is only spoiled goodness. . . . you must first have the idea of [normality] before you can talk of its being perverted; and you can see which is the perversion, because you can explain the perverted from the normal, and cannot explain the normal from the perverted." Lewis also adds, "[E]vil is a parasite, not an original thing."[1]

Satan cannot create; he can only pervert. Everything that is holy and right in a relationship between a parent and child is defined by God and purposefully undermined, attacked, and mangled by Satan.

When it comes to discipline, we must set a proper template for our children so they can understand what is good and normal and just and right.

---

1. C.S. Lewis, *Mere Christianity* (New York, NY: Harper Collins, 2001), p. 44–45.

Sinful Children and Sinful Parents

All of us would like to think we are exempt from committing sinful acts simply because we are "good" people. God's Word is emphatic that no one is born naturally good.

> The heart is deceitful above all things, and desperately sick; who can understand it? (Jer. 17:9).

> Surely I was sinful at birth, sinful from the time my mother conceived me (Ps. 51:5; NIV).

> And Jesus said to him, "Why do you call me good? No one is good except God alone" (Mark 10:18).

We must come to grips with the fact that any of us can fail and commit sin against another person. The more convinced we are of our own moral goodness, the more prone we are to fall.

> Therefore let anyone who thinks that he stands take heed lest he fall (1 Cor. 10:12).

> When pride comes, then comes disgrace, but with the humble is wisdom (Prov. 11:2).

We see the sinful behavior in our child's heart as expressed through his or her actions.

> For all have sinned and fall short of the glory of God (Rom. 3:23).

> Therefore, just as sin came into the world through one man, and death through sin, and so death spread to all men because all sinned (Rom. 5:12).

Yes, our children are sinners, but when we discipline, we need to remember that God is still trying to root out our own fleshly nature as well. We should be humble in our discipline in realizing that we are not where we need to be either.

Selfishness

We live in a society that promotes self-gratification. As opposed to the scriptural mandate to deny ourselves (doesn't that concept sound outdated?!), we are told that we deserve to do something for ourselves. Men are told they have a right to their free time and should have space for their personal interests. Children, by nature of their vulnerability, tend to encroach on a father's desire to unwind and kick back after the hectic pace of a stressful work week. Children need their fathers. Children have legitimate needs that they are unable to meet by themselves. There becomes a competition between the perceived needs of the father and the pressing needs of the child or children. Someone will have to be denied. It is a rare father who will deny himself to care for the needs of the children entrusted to him.

Society teaches mothers that their only value is found in being a career woman, and their identity must be proven outside the home. They are taught that, if they truly love their children, they will place them in daycare and let the professionals handle the tough job of child-rearing. Some women even convince themselves that they are sacrificing for the good of the child. However, it is not normal for a mother to abandon the care of her own offspring to another person, no matter how noble it may appear.

The worldview that insists she "owes it to herself" to put her own life and career above the needs of her child is logically similar to the argument that she has a "right" to abort her own child. It is a total violation of the natural order. I'm not addressing the actual issue of women working outside the home (sometimes that is a valid economic necessity). I am comparing the logic that the "life of the mother" is somehow intrinsically more valuable than the life of the child. A normal mother will do everything in her power (even give up her own physical life) to ensure that the life of the child is preserved. We cannot call ourselves Christians if we refuse to deny ourselves and lay down our lives. In some cases, a mother lays down her life by getting a necessary job away from her children to feed, clothe, and shelter them. For many in our self-centered culture, however, mothers are told to put their desires first and not allow anything (even their own children) to stand in the way of her own happiness or self-expression. This is not a biblical worldview.

How can we teach our children not to be selfish if our entire lifestyle is predicated on us putting ourselves first at the expense of legitimate emotional needs of our own children? Obviously, there is a balance in all things. Self-care is legitimate. You need to make sure you are emotionally and physically as healthy as you can be in order to properly care for children. But our me-first generation flies in the face of biblical Christianity, which declares:

> Let each of you look not only to his own interests,
> but also to the interests of others (Phil. 2:4).

Anger and Stress

Because Brook and I care so much about the devastating harm anger has on children, we wrote an entire book on the topic. *Pitchin' A Fit! Overcoming Angry & Stressed-Out Parenting* is a comprehensive look at a biblical and practical view of anger and stress.

There are many causes for anger, but regardless of why a parent is angry, the child often receives the negative impact of the parent's frustration. Many Christian parents try to hide their ungodly attitudes and fleshly responses under the religious garb of "righteous indignation." The Bible says, "Because human anger does not produce the righteousness that God desires" (James 1:20; NIV). If you want to bring about the righteousness of God in your children, you will not accomplish it through the wrath of man.

Galatians 6:7 says we will reap what we sow. If we sow seeds of anger in the life of our child, we will reap anger, bitterness, and rejection. Outbursts of anger are in the "works of the flesh" column in Galatians 5, not the fruit of the Spirit. John 3:6 tells us that "the Spirit gives birth to spirit" (NIV). If we want a spiritual outcome, we need to use a spiritual method.

We all know Proverbs 22:15, "Foolishness is bound up in the heart of a child; The rod of correction will drive it far from him" (NKJV). This verse, earlier in the same chapter, is lesser known: Proverbs 22:8, "Whoever sows injustice will reap calamity, and the rod of his fury will fail." There is nothing righteous about a parent simply being ticked off and taking it out on a child. The problem is the anger with which parents respond toward their children. Anger is a destroyer.

Obviously, when a child does something wrong or destructive, a parent should express his or her displeasure. I'm not suggesting that we should approve of everything our children do. I'm not insinuating that we should pretend to be happy all the time, even when we are deeply troubled or grieved at the behavior of our children. But I am saying it is not our place to vent our wrath on our children, making them take the brunt of our frustration. A parent who is not self-disciplined will likely discipline his or her own children improperly.

Taking your anger out on your child is never excusable. Many parents would never physically harm their child; however, they are still sinning against their child if they verbally berate him or her or pour out their anger against him or her. Hurtful words can be emotionally devastating to a child.

A child should have a healthy respect for his or her parents and should expect that defiance and disobedience will be met with correction and discipline. There should be no doubt in the child's mind that the parents' instructions must be obeyed. What a tragedy, however, for a child to cower in fear, quaking in terror because of the unpredictable rage and fury of an uncontrolled parental temper tantrum. Children should long to be with their parents, and they should not feel relieved when the parent is gone. Children who experience loving, godly, biblical discipline usually love and respect their parents and want to be around them. A child who flinches at an unexpected motion of a parent is often indicating that they are not being disciplined in a biblical manner.

A Loss of Shame

Selfishness leads to a justification of anger, which leads in turn to a searing of the conscience. Once our hearts are no longer tender to the correcting and rebuking word of truth, we become desensitized and hardened to sin. We justify our harmful actions against others by telling ourselves that our actions are not what they appear to be. I have known abusers and alcoholics who insist that they don't have a problem. They have convinced themselves that their actions don't negatively affect others. They are still in control and everything is fine.

In his book *Deliver Us from Evil*, Ravi Zacharias explains, "The unbearable reality of secularism's consequential loss of shame is that the ones we victimize by evil can even be the ones we claim to love. . . . This is the crime we end up witnessing when family members kill their own offspring. . . . To remove shame is to perpetuate evil even towards the ones we love. The catalog of crimes between families . . . is one of the most painful and most incomprehensible. The evils we foist upon children at the hands of responsible adults are not crimes born of hate. They are passions unleashed and justified by a conscience bereft of shame or remorse. Any conversation with a police officer who investigates criminality within families reveals horror stories that stun the mind. Almost every police officer I have met has said to me that if we were to know even a fraction of all that goes on in homes behind closed doors the knowledge would be heartbreaking. Shame is meant to protect the very ones we love. But our culture has killed it. With the Name of God now unhallowed and His Kingdom not welcome does it make any sense to cry, 'Deliver us from evil'?"[2]

Failures

Improper discipline runs on a continuum that stretches from the dysfunctional to the truly evil. A parent who "blows a fuse" ranting and raving; storming around the house; taunting; provoking; intimidating; verbally berating and belittling; throwing things; grabbing their child by the arm and yanking them around; shaking them; pulling their hair; slapping them; pushing them; kicking them; purposefully depriving them of needed food, sleep, or basic clothing; throwing them around in anger; or randomly hitting them with sticks or other objects is totally inappropriate.

Mistreatment of children can take on extreme forms that boggle the mind in the depths of their evil. We obviously can't list every possible form of mistreatment, but suffice it to say that anything

---

2. Ravi Zacharias, *Deliver Us From Evil* (Dallas, TX: Word Publishing, 1996), p. 66.

that surpasses the hideous sins we have already described, including any form of sexual abuse, is an abomination that cannot be justified in any way.

> And he said to his disciples, "Temptations to sin are sure to come, but woe to the one through whom they come! It would be better for him if a millstone were hung around his neck and he were cast into the sea than that he should cause one of these little ones to sin" (Luke 17:1–2).

Can You Change Bad Patterns?

If you realize that you have been abusive to your child in any way (especially if it is a chronic pattern), you need to repent, immediately stop your inappropriate behavior, and seek professional therapy. You need to learn how to biblically discipline your child, and that will likely involve seeking out counsel from those who are mature followers of Christ. You need to repent to your children for your anger, your selfishness, and your failure to use your position of leadership responsibly. Humble yourself before your children and request their forgiveness. Commit before them that by God's grace you want to be a godly parent. Explain to them what you have done that is inappropriate and tell them how things will change (so they will know what to expect). Learn to be predictable and consistent in training your children. Children do not thrive on chaos and confusion.

If you have a problem with anger, God may choose not to deliver you overnight, but you must stop your inappropriate behavior immediately. You need to learn, through God's Word, perhaps professional therapy, and the counsel of mature Christians who can keep you accountable, how to overcome anger so it doesn't control you anymore. Again, we would refer you to our book on that topic as well, as God has used it to help transform thousands of families.

Chapter 10

Be the Parent

Behold, children are a heritage from the LORD, the
fruit of the womb a reward (Ps. 127:3).

On the one hand, parenting is the most difficult task you will ever
undertake. If you think you are equipped to be a good parent, think
again. You aren't. You are in over your head. You have been given a
task that is beyond your means and abilities. So that's the bad news.

The good news, on the other hand, is that you are not alone. If
you belong to Christ, the God of the universe is in covenant partnership with you in raising these children. It is He who placed these
precious children into your hands and home. Actually, biblically
speaking, these children belong to Him (Ps. 127), and He rewards
us by allowing us to be caretakers and stewards of HIS children.
Because they don't belong to us, but to Him, we need to find out
what He expects of us and how He wants us to raise His children.

Have you ever watched someone else's children for them? If
so, you understand that you ask the parents how they want you
to care for their children. What foods do they allow their children
to eat? What games are they allowed to play? When do they take a
nap? When is their bedtime? As a caretaker or steward, we can't just
do anything we like. We can't treat them any way we want to. We
need to do what the parents want us to do. Since God is our child's
ultimate authority, we're not permitted to make arbitrary decisions
concerning our children. We need to find out what God desires for
His children. How does HE want HIS children to be raised?

The good thing is that He is not silent. He has given us a wealth of knowledge and direction in His Word about parenting, education, and child training. As partners with Him in raising His children, He doesn't expect us to be perfect parents. He does, however, expect us to give 100% of our heart to this process. If we look to Him, God will give us wisdom and understanding about how to do this job in a way that pleases Him (see James 1:5).

In addition to studying Scripture, God has also commanded us to be connected to healthy Christian community through a local church. Guidance from biblically qualified church elders can help us learn how to take the commands we find in Scripture and apply them wisely in the context of child-rearing. It is important that we find a church where the leaders meet the criteria described in 1 Timothy 3 and Titus 1, because if they do, they will have the wisdom needed to help guide us in our parenting journey.

Basic Ground Rules

There are a few basic guidelines that will make a world of difference in terms of your effectiveness in being a good parent.

You Are the Parent, They Are the Children

It's alarming how many Christian parents haven't figured out this basic premise. They have a three-year-old who runs the house, and the parents live in abject frustration because of the tyranny of a child who refuses to obey.

It has always been my goal to stand firm when our small children (inevitably) test our authority through defiance and rebellion. It is just not best for these precious little children to be allowed to rule our home. They need to learn a proper place of obedience to their parents.

I've seen three-year-olds who won't come to their parents when called. The parent says, "Come to Daddy!" and the child turns and runs the other way. Oftentimes the parents laugh it off, thinking it is cute. What happens if the child starts to chase a ball into the road and the parent sees an oncoming car? If he or she calls to the child to stop and the child has always been allowed to ignore and defy the parent's instructions, that child can be killed. Teaching obedience is not merely for the convenience of the parent, it is imperative to protect that child's life!

> Children, obey your parents in everything, for this pleases the Lord (Col. 3:20).

Achieving the goal of consistent obedience from your child is a difficult task! You need to plan on investing huge sums of time into parenting if you want to establish a clear understanding in your child's mind regarding who is in charge. Just having this goal in mind before our children were born made a huge difference in how we approached parenting. Letting the child "win" the authority battle is simply not an option — ever. It makes parenting much easier once it is clear in your own mind just who is in charge. Being the authority figure does not mean being an ogre. Jesus taught servant leadership. He was patient and gentle with His disciples. He still instructed them to obey what He told them and expected them to do it. "If you love me, obey my commandments" (John 14:15; NLT).

Someone asked me recently if we have ever had a strong-willed child. I replied, "Yes, all of them." While I understand that some children are far more naturally defiant than others, all children want to get their own way. Every child who has ever been born has a strong will (even the seemingly compliant ones); they just express their wills in different ways (some less overt, and some less obvious at various ages). Obviously, children with developmental challenges may act in ways that make them seem "strong-willed," but those children will need to be approached with more patience than a child with normal cognitive development.

When your children are between ages 2 to 10, they often test the boundaries to see who is in charge. If you haven't established respect from your children by age 10, you are going to really struggle in the tween and teen years. Too many parents want so badly to be liked by their children, but here's the deal: children don't respect parents who are afraid of them (and therefore, they don't like them much either). Don't make being your young child's buddy your chief goal. Be the parent. Be firm and consistent. There are plenty of ways to have fun, show love, cuddle with, read to, and be a blessing to your children without letting them rule over you. When you give them an instruction, they don't have to like it. They just need to do it. Once they understand and know that disobedience and defiance is never an option, they will settle in and enjoy life.

Children Need Boundaries

Children can't handle having unlimited possibilities. Children thrive on security, predictability, order, structure, and boundaries, not on chaos and randomness. Some parents think they are stifling their child's creativity or "free spirit" by creating rules and boundaries for him or her. The greatest creativity always flows from structure. Great concert pianists, who play with the greatest ease and whose fingers float effortlessly over the ivories, are the ones who have spent thousands of painstaking hours learning the form and intricate methods of music technique. The truly great painters produce masterpieces because of how well they understand the geometry and mathematics of art and obey the rules of symmetry.

As a general guideline, children should have routines. Structure can, of course, be overdone. We've all met parents who need to learn to lighten up a bit and let their children be children. But in general, children need to have basic times when they get up in the morning, when they go to sleep, when they eat, and when they do their studies. They need to know what Mom and Dad expect from them.

What Does It Mean to Train? (Brook)

One of the definitions that Noah Webster gives in his 1828 Dictionary for the word "train" gives so much insight for us as parents. Train: "to teach and form by practice." This definition has really helped me in knowing how to go about imparting what I have in my mind to my children. This aspect of forming, by practice, is a key component in knowing just when to expect obedience from our children on a particular instruction. Every child will vary greatly, both in his or her physical ability to perform certain tasks and in the willingness to lay aside his or her own desires to be obedient! In a wide sweeping fashion, then, children roughly under the age of five will need a good deal of practice in the small basics of life before you can speak once and expect your words to be obeyed. These little ones need you to get right in the mix and help them make their bed, put their shoes away, or pick up the toys. When you see they have become capable of performing the function, begin a transition process whereby you begin directing your child to go about the task on his or her own. This practice training can give you the confidence you need to adequately know when to expect obedience. This kind of practice works well for attitude problems, and manners, too!

Key Components for Training

Through my mothering years, I've often sought solutions to parenting dilemmas, hoping my search would produce the perfect answer for each situation. I think there must be a lot of parents out there like me because I have had many conversations with parents who are also looking for a magic cure for their children doing things like arguing, name-calling, complaining, lying, stealing, hitting, bullying, and so much more. There are definitely specific Scriptures that will apply directly to each of these temptations, but I'd like to offer a bit of a template that could apply to any one of these specific problems.

Lay out clear and simple teaching ahead of time. This is where quantitative proactive time snuggling on the couch, enjoying the swings together at the park, or eating giant bowls of ice cream comes in. We have an imperative from the Lord (in Deuteronomy 6:7) to get "ahead of the game," so to speak, and talk with our children about life matters before the actual need arises. Let's say you (randomly) pick the importance of speaking the truth. Talk with your crew about why God's people must not lie. Speak about the consequences and harm to relationships and trust that comes through lying. Use story books, make up silly songs, memorize key Bible verses. You are laying a foundation of understanding and a roadmap for your children.

Practice. Ask questions. Often, young children fall into bad habits relationally when they don't know how to act or what to do, or in a scenario that takes them by surprise. Give them an edge by role-playing and rehearsing what they would do in situations where they would have to choose between right and wrong. Practice real-life scenarios, like what to do when your sister hits you, what to do when your friend wants to tell you a secret, what to do when your parents call you away from a game to empty the dishwasher, how to receive instruction when a parent says "no" to a certain book, etc.

Don't be surprised when they sin. Our children are made of the same human flesh we are and will struggle and fail in their journey. When this happens, don't be shocked, even though it may be personally painful, inconvenient, or embarrassing. Rise above your feelings in the matter and walk them through the needed discipline and repentance. Children don't naturally know how to receive correction. Most of the time, they need to be led in how to be "teachable." Don't just hand out negative consequences. Walk them through how to humble themselves, how to pray for courage to do right in the future, and how to go about the difficult prospect of making things right. While simultaneously upholding truth and righteousness by God's grace, we also need to strive to reflect the amazing love of God toward sinful children. That kind of attitude never ignores or makes light of sin, but it does provide a stance of receiving the repentant sinner.

Pray to see the root issues. Sometimes the unpleasant attitudes we see on the surface only reflect a deeper heart issue. We may try to clean up the outside of our children's demeanors all we like, but until our children open up for God to do a work on the heart issue, our work is just going to continue on and on. Sibling rivalry is largely made up of this kind of stuff. First it is a squabble, then a disagreeable attitude, followed by someone pestering the other and loud complaints. It is all terribly unpleasant, and for a bit of peace and quiet, we parents are often quick to try to trim at the weeds we see so they are less visible. But just like a nasty weed, it will crop up with fresh vigor and strength just as soon as the sun shines on it again. As parents, we need to be astute enough to realize there IS a deeper root, take time to search the Scriptures to find wisdom, and pray that God will grant us eyes to see how we can help our children.

Spend a lot of time together. All this teaching and talking and discussing and practicing needs time, lots of it. That's exactly why we're so into encouraging you as a parent to be fully engaged in your family. If your children are home with you during the day, you'll get some great training moments, and you can probably find even more if you are more intentional. A lot of these teaching moments come out of simply doing life together, perhaps even when you least expect it. A few seconds at a stoplight or while you are hurriedly throwing dinner together. Or while you are cleaning out your car. If you are there, and you are together, those moments for sharing your faith, for passing on the meaning of life, for noticing and praising a cheerful attitude, are available for you to take and use. Just as important, when we're truly present with our families, we'll be there to ward off wrong and sinful habits as they crop up, many times before they become more deeply rooted problems.

When your children are away from you at school, you don't see those moments when their anger flares in frustration, the unkind words they speak, or the lies they tell. You can only train in the moment if your children are with you.

Perhaps this is precisely why the Bible doesn't lay out instant formulas for parenting success. The answer is relationship. If we could give our children a pill that would instantaneously fix their whining and complaining, we wouldn't need to hang in with them, working through the messiness of ugly attitudes and difficult conversations. In fact, the whole of the parenting experience would require much less involvement. In reality, when we get "stuck" and reach an impasse in our child — a struggle within — we must plead with God our Father for wisdom and insight into our child. It is an ongoing work of teaching our child the truth, helping him or her see right from wrong, praying for the Holy Spirit to bring conviction, and walking with him or her in the path of repentance.

Galatians 6:1 gives incredible advice: "Brothers and sisters, if someone is caught in a sin, you who live by the Spirit should restore that person gently. But watch yourselves, or you also may be tempted" (NIV). This is, of course, speaking to those within the Church, but it is also prescriptive for us as parents. This is what happens, isn't it? We catch our children in sin. That means we must be there to do that catching! And then it says we need to restore them. Gently. You will be thrown a lot of curveballs in your parenting adventure. There will be situations you don't know how to handle, problems you don't know how to cure. When you are there, remember this verse and choose to first of all walk in the Spirit and, secondly, see to restoring your child.

Predictable Consequences (Israel)

Children need to have predictable consequences if they are lazy, sloppy, disobedient, mean to a sibling, or backtalking their parents. They have difficulty handling a situation where Mom deals with things one way and Dad deals with them in an opposite way. They can't make sense of random behavior where Mom flies off the handle for something on Tuesday, ignores the same offense on Wednesday, and has a completely different reaction on Thursday for the same misbehavior.

Children feel a tremendous sense of security from knowing that Mom and Dad love them, that Mom and Dad love each other, that they are safe, that they will be provided for, and that their parents care enough to tell them no (and mean it!). They need to know their parents will follow through with appropriate consequences and consistent parenting when they disobey.

Discipline Should Not Be Erratic

I will sometimes tell my children, "If you do not put your game away after you are finished playing it, I will take away the game for a week. If you want to be able to access your games, you need to exercise responsibility that is appropriate to the privilege. This will be the case for all your games. If you leave them out, you won't be allowed to play them for a week. Do you understand?"

This gives my children a predictable consequence that incentivizes them to practice responsibility. They know what to expect. If the game is off limits for a week because of their negligence, that is on them. Since I've set up the boundary ahead of time, there are no surprises. This helps to reduce conflict. As long as I am consistent in applying the discipline, they will learn that they also need to be consistent.

Value Your Words

Do your words mean anything to you? They should. If you give your child an instruction, value your own words to them. If you don't really intend for your child to make his or her bed, don't bother telling him or her to do it. Just make the bed yourself. However, if you really, genuinely want your son or daughter to make his or her own bed, then you had better value your words enough to make sure that it happens. Provide some guidelines so your child knows when he or she is supposed to accomplish this (e.g., "You need to have your bed made in the next 15 minutes before breakfast"), give a predictable consequence if it doesn't happen, and then follow through with it as necessary.

If I am giving my son an instruction, I will usually do the following: I will say, "Son, I need you to go and pick up all of the whiffle balls in the yard and put them away. Do you understand?"

"OK."

"Good. What do I want you to do?"

"I don't know." (He wasn't really listening. I tell him again.)

"You want me to pick up all the whiffle balls in the yard and put them away."

"Correct. Do it right away."

"Yes, sir."

We always require our young children to say, "Yes, sir," or "Yes, ma'am," when they are given an instruction. It lets us know they are attentive and responsive. (If that sounds too formal for you, that's fine. Use whatever you are comfortable with but do require a verbal response.) When they fail to answer appropriately, or with an appropriate tone of voice, it usually indicates that they are having a sour attitude and their hearts are not with us. We then address the attitude before returning to the instruction at hand.

Discipline Is Not Punishment

> Train up a child in the way he should go; even when he is old he will not depart from it (Prov. 22:6).

Our goal is to train our children, not punish them.

> There is no fear in love, but perfect love casts out fear. For fear has to do with punishment, and whoever fears has not been perfected in love (1 John 4:18).

Our children should have a proper respect for us but should never cower in fear of their parents. They need to know their parents' decisions are in the best interests of the children rather than punishments for crossing their parents in some way. Prisons punish those who do wrong, but they rarely teach proper behavior.

Our goal with discipline should always be for the good of the child (Heb. 12:10) and never for our own selfish desire to repay our child for an offense or making our lives inconvenient. We need to discipline them to train them in the right direction.

Absolutely Consistent Follow-Through

When you have given a clear instruction to your child and confirmed he or she heard you, you need to ensure he or she follows through with obedience. When a child has heard you and repeated back the instruction to you, he or she is now responsible for completing the required instruction. At this point, the child is not allowed to use the excuses of "I didn't hear you" (he or she repeated the command, so you know he or she did) or "I forgot." When you asked your son to pick up the whiffle balls in the backyard and you find him five minutes later playing with toys in the living room (his task left undone), he needs to receive an expected discipline. You shouldn't argue with him, yell, or create drama. You should simply discipline him and explain that he needs to respect your words.

"I Forgot"

As I was reading through the Old Testament, seeing how God interacted with the children of Israel, I was struck by how many times He told them not to forget what He was telling them. He told them to write it down on their foreheads and doorposts (Deut. 6) and to build altars of remembrance (Josh. 4:1–7).

Not remembering God's words is a sin. "So whoever knows the right thing to do and fails to do it, for him it is sin" (James 4:17). It shows a disregard for, and dishonor toward, God's words. We need to value God's words, not take them lightly or treat them glibly. Romans 1:28 (KJV) says people in rebellion to God "did not like to retain God in their knowledge." We need to retain God's words.

In a similar way, our children need to retain our words. It is part of honoring their father and mother (Exod. 20:12). My children always remember my words if I tell them something that is important to them. They will never forget if I promise to buy them ice cream or take them to the park. They only seem to forget when they are told to do something they don't enjoy. They tend to hear, and retain, what they deem to be important (usually what is fun). But they need to learn to esteem what is important to their parents and not merely what is important to them. If they have been given instruction (and repeated it back) yet fail to follow through, they need consistent follow-through with discipline. No arguing, complaining, or excusing should be tolerated. If they are always given prompt discipline, they will learn that they need to consider Mom and Dad's words to be important.

Train Their Hearts, Not Just Their Behavior

Parenting is not about producing some kind of predictable Pavlovian or Skinnerian behavior from our children. We are not training them like laboratory rats to respond to positive or negative stimuli. Our desire is that we have our children's hearts. We want them to be fully participating on the family team.

Successful biblical parenting is not the Marines. It is not about children dutifully saying "Yes, ma'am" and obeying barked-out orders yet hating their parents in their hearts. Anger, bitter words, deceit, meanness, sulking, pouting, complaining, etc., are all works of the flesh (see Gal. 5). We want our children to learn how to walk in the Spirit. Our goal is to raise children who love God (and their parents) from their hearts. We want them to have a dynamic relationship with God (and with us) and to serve out of a heart of love, not out of mere duty and obligation. If they don't "feel the love" at a given moment, that's okay. They can just obey anyway and wait for the warm fuzzies to come back later. We are helping them to live servant-hearted lives. We are training them to think not of themselves only, but also of the needs of others (1 Pet. 4:10). Obedience trains them to say no to themselves, which creates good soil in their hearts for the seeds of the Spirit to later grow.

Throw Yourself on the Mercy of God

One of my great heroes of the faith is a 19th-century Dutch Reformed missionary to South Africa named Andrew Murray. This man of God wrote many wonderful books, including *The Believer's Absolute Surrender; With Christ in the School of Prayer; Holiness; With Christ in the School of Obedience; Abiding in Christ;* and many others. He and his wife, Emma, were godly parents of eight children who all grew up serving the Lord as missionaries or pastors or as wives of missionaries or pastors.

In his book on parenting, *Raising Your Children to Love Christ,* Murray talks about our inadequacies as parents. I will summarize some of his thoughts for you. He says that as a parent you want to teach, train, disciple, correct, instruct, challenge, rebuke, encourage, praise, and lead your child. You do absolutely everything you can to help this child know and love God. At the end of it all, however, there are some things that you just can't do for your child. You need to do everything you can to keep your end of the covenant with God in this child-raising process. However, doing the best you can do is not enough. Your best efforts will still fall short. You are an imperfect parent, and you will make mistakes.

So, what do you do? Give up? Admit defeat? No, not at all! Remember that God loves HIS children more than you ever could and that He has so much invested in them. If you have done everything you can, to the best of your ability, then throw yourself on the mercy of God and plead for Him to make up for your lack. Cry out to God and ask Him to do in your child's heart and mind what you cannot accomplish. Ask Him to create circumstances that will direct this child to surrendering his or her life to Christ.

When you do this, do it with a full heart of confidence, knowing that God will move heaven and earth to keep His part of the covenant, if you have been faithful in your part. You are not alone in this parenting process. You are not even the most important component. The Spirit of the living God is also at work, and you are in partnership with that Spirit. Look to Christ at every turn. Seek Him and His wisdom daily. Turn to Him and let Him lead you every step of the journey. You can't do this alone, but the good news is, you aren't expected to!

Chapter 11

Child Discipline

Does the Child Require Discipline?

One of the concerns many parents have with discipline is knowing when a child is aware enough of the situation to warrant discipline. Here are some guidelines.

Age

When you give instruction to a toddler, and he or she turns around, looks you in the eye, and defiantly says, "No, I don't want to!" you are ready to start correcting that child. The child knows what he or she wants, and it is to do the opposite of what you are instructing.

When your teenager is driving a car and comes home at 11:30 p.m. instead of the agreed-upon 10:00 p.m., that teen is ready to be disciplined. The parent may rightly remove driving privileges for a week. In general, it's pretty obvious when a child is aware of the situation and needs to receive discipline.

Developmental Delays

Where this becomes more difficult is when a child has some kind of developmental brain delays, emotional scarring from trauma, or other special needs or learning disabilities that put the child into a different emotional category than his or her age would ordinarily suggest. In situations like this, we encourage parents to pursue a medical/clinical diagnosis and follow advice from a medical or developmental professional.

Physical Considerations

One thing my wife and I highly recommend is having your child regularly evaluated by a family physician who can keep tabs on the development of your child. It is wise to have all your children evaluated for hearing and vision and tested for possible food allergies. While none of these issues alone exclusively dictate behavior, it is imperative to know if there are limitations on your child's ability to understand and respond appropriately.

As an example, one of our children was constantly saying, "I didn't hear you say that," when given an instruction. We took him to several hearing tests and were told his hearing was fine. We felt something was still amiss, so we took him to a hearing specialist who tested him and diagnosed him with Auditory Processing Disorder. He could hear the sounds fine in his ear, but the information got jumbled up in his brain, and he became disoriented. We were taught that we could take him into another room where there were no distracting stimuli, give him the instruction, have him repeat it back to us, and he would follow through. It was a simple solution but one we would not have understood without a proper diagnosis. We may have blamed him for being rebellious when it was merely a physical issue.

The same is true for a child who can't see properly. Without corrective lenses, he or she may perform poorly in school and be wrongly blamed for being lazy or not trying hard enough. It may be a simple solution that eyeglasses can fix.

If a child is allergic to dairy or has celiac disease, it may impact his or her mood, which in turn affects behavior. It is not true that all behavioral problems are rooted in our bodies. Each child has a will and can choose at any point to be defiant. We don't believe that every behavioral issue can be solved with merely a good diet or essential oils. It does make sense, however, to explore any possible physical limitations of the child before beginning the work on his or her mind, emotions, and spirit. It makes the relational journey easier when the child's body is functioning at an optimum level.

Appropriate Correction

When a child is disobedient, rebellious, or defiant, a wise and normal parent will share with him or her that what he or she has done is wrong, and the parent will be faithful to apply a previously explained equal consequence or correction that considers the child's age, maturity, and any developmental challenges. It is also important to consider personality. Some children are more receptive to discipline than others. For one child, a simple look may be enough for him or her to quit the negative behavior. For others, they may need a time out or a loss of a privilege. Parents are the best ones to make these decisions because they know each child better than anyone else and can customize the discipline to each child and situation.

> And have you forgotten the exhortation that addresses you as sons? "My son, do not regard lightly the discipline of the Lord, nor be weary when reproved by him. For the Lord disciplines the one he loves, and chastises every son whom he receives." It is for discipline that you have to endure. God is treating you as sons. For what son is there whom his father does not discipline? If you are left without discipline, in which all have participated, then you are illegitimate children and not sons. Besides this, we have had earthly fathers who disciplined us and we respected them. Shall we not much more be subject to the Father of spirits and live? For they disciplined us for a short time as it seemed best to them, but he disciplines us for our good, that we may share his holiness. For the moment all discipline seems painful rather than pleasant, but later it yields the peaceful fruit of righteousness to those who have been trained by it (Heb. 12:5–11).

A parent who consistently administers discipline to his or her child from a young age will probably never have to worry about turning his or her relationship with the child into an emotional wrestling match. The child will soon learn to receive correction without resentment.

A parent should never be out of control, yelling or speaking to a child with clenched teeth or bitter words. After following through with discipline, wise parents will comfort their disciplined children, holding them close, praying with them, helping them to ask God for forgiveness for their sin, expressing their love once again, and reassuring them of their place of fellowship within the family.

A child should never have just cause to feel like a parent hates him or her, is taking out his or her anger through discipline, or just wants to get even in some way. Discipline is always and only for the good of the child. It is a mercy to our children when it is utilized correctly and lovingly.

Dad Should Be the Driving Force in Discipline

It was a great revelation to me some years ago when I realized in my Bible study that every single passage in the Bible that speaks about discipline either mentioned the concept generically or, in most cases, directed the command to fathers. I haven't found one verse in the entire Bible (Old or New Testament) where God ever commands a mother to discipline a child! I think that is significant. Mothers end up doing the bulk of child discipline, and they often feel burnt out and frustrated with the lack of results. I know that in our own family, we gained some wonderful results once I took over my place of leadership on this issue.

As a married couple, we are co-heirs of the grace of life (see 1 Pet. 3:7). We share parenting duties, and one parent is not excluded by God from any facet of the parenting process. But the Bible does not give equal instruction or equal weight of responsibility on all matters to both fathers and mothers. There are occasions when one parent is given a stronger admonition in the parenting role. This is true for fathers in both teaching and discipline. More passages directly command fathers to teach than mothers, and Scripture puts a supreme emphasis on fathers disciplining children.

When there is a situation where a father is unwilling or unable to discipline a child, for whatever reason, then the duty may fall exclusively to mothers. I've heard of some cases where a father, because of an anger issue, chooses not to discipline because he is overly harsh. There are also situations where a woman is a single parent or must function as one. In such cases, mothers may need to take up the slack. But I have found this frequently creates an enormous amount of stress for mothers, especially when their sons approach and enter puberty. Young men at that age especially need their fathers (in an ideal scenario) to handle discipline issues. When a father is not in the picture (at least not in a significant way), the task for the mother is much more difficult but not impossible (as my own story can attest).

The Discipline Chart

I have learned that in most cases, if there is a problem with one of our children disrespecting their mother or having a hardened heart, it is usually because I have become negligent in relationship and discipline with my children. My wife is a great mom and does a fabulous job, so when things aren't working, it's usually because I'm not leading. I'm not saying this is true for every family, but it is for ours, at least so far.

When our oldest children were about seven, six, four, two, and a baby, my wife lamented to me that she was simply not getting anything done because the children were disobeying her all day. She said, "If I disciplined these children or fussed at them every time they disobeyed me, ignored my words, or defied me, I'd do nothing else!"

I knew I needed wisdom. So, I prayed about it. The next day, I created "The Discipline Chart." Now, before you follow this method, I'm not saying this is what every parent should do. This is just what we did because I felt the Lord was leading me to do it.

The Discipline Chart had three boxes. Suppose my wife told our six-year-old to sweep the kitchen floor (one of her chores), and she instead went off to play with Legos® with her brother. My wife would lead her over to the refrigerator door and put a pen in her hand, and my daughter would place an "X" in the first box. The first two boxes represented a predictable loss of a privilege that the child enjoyed. So, the first box might be a loss of dessert after dinner that night. My wife would write the specific disobedience over the box so I could discuss it with my daughter when I returned from work.

The next box might be not getting to listen to an audio story that night at bedtime. I think it is important to have the child check the box him or herself because it is a way of taking responsibility for what he or she did. The child needs to check that box with his or her own hand.

The third box, though, was altogether different. If I came home and found three boxes checked, I would give that child an age-appropriate consequence.

For the first week, every child maxed out the chart every day. We only did this with the older three because the two-year-old needed immediate correction if he did something disobedient. His little mind was not developed enough to remember something he had done ten minutes ago, let alone six hours before. Our four-year-old was old enough to remember his actions from earlier in the day and was mentally mature enough to explain to me what he had done and why it was wrong, so he was included.

The deal was that my wife shouldn't discipline at all during the day unless there was an urgent need. She shouldn't argue with the children, raise her voice, fuss at them, threaten them with loss of privileges, etc. As soon as a child disobeyed, he or she went immediately to the refrigerator and made an "X." It was kind of a "three strikes and you're out" method in that every infraction after the third box would be included in the conversation we had when I got home and disciplined them.

As I said, we did this every day for a week. I would discipline them, and they didn't like it. My wife's life was already getting better because she had stopped stressing. The weight was no longer on her shoulders, but rather on mine, where it belonged. Discipline is primarily Dad's job (when he is available and willing to do it). I'm not saying that a mother is not allowed to discipline her children. By no means. In fact, she needed to correct the two-year-old for his own safety. A very young child won't remember bad things he or she did earlier in the day, so he or she needs to be corrected right away by the mother. I'm just saying that Mom is Dad's helpmeet, not the other way around. (See Gen. 2:18 and 1 Cor. 11:8–9.)

After one week, none of my children would go past two marks on the chart. For the next month, they regularly got two marks right off the bat, but then they would dig in their heels and absolutely refuse to allow themselves that third disobedience or defiance. I was amazed. I was committed to this process for the long haul. I thought they might continue the same negative behavior for months or even years! I was surprised how relatively quickly things turned around.

My wife was so much more productive, and our home was so much more peaceful. I was finally taking responsibility for discipline, even though I was working outside the home. I had been involved before that, but it was realizing that discipline wasn't my wife's primary job that helped us find success. I thought that because I was at work for long hours of the day and didn't want to be a big ogre at night when I came home, I simply couldn't be the lead disciplinarian. I was wrong.

Eventually, the children had fewer and fewer marks on the chart overall. I believe the change was not because my discipline was any different than that administered by my wife or that my children were intimidated by me. Neither was true. The deal was that neither I nor my children enjoyed spending our precious time together that way. They didn't want Dad to be unhappy with them. They didn't want to have to tell Dad all the bad things they did that day. They didn't want Dad, whom they loved and wanted to do fun things with, spending his home time disciplining them. It was a relationship issue.

Children want attention. They'll settle for negative attention if that is all they can get, but they respond much more positively to positive attention. They thrived on my coming home and making a big fuss about how happy I was that I didn't need to discipline them. They beamed when I told them how pleased I was that they were learning to be good helpers to their mother.

Parents who don't discipline their children often become frustrated because they have no viable means of restraining their child or making their child obey them. These parents usually live at a very high stress level (as do parents who discipline in a wrong way). Failure to discipline a child almost always results in a child whose behavior no one likes or wants to be around.

Discipline is essential because God requires it of you, but it must be applied with prayer and wisdom. It is only when you are in alignment with His Spirit of love and self-restraint that you will be able to see the proper fruit from its application.

What Does the Bible Say?

Here are just a few of the many, many passages on discipline in the Bible:

> My son, do not despise the LORD's discipline or be weary of his reproof, for the LORD reproves him whom he loves, as a father the son in whom he delights (Prov. 3:11–12).

> Whoever spares the rod hates his son, but he who loves him is diligent to discipline him (Prov. 13:24).

> Discipline your son, for there is hope; do not set your heart on putting him to death (Prov. 19:18).

> Folly is bound up in the heart of a child, but the rod of discipline drives it far from him (Prov. 22:15).

> Do not withhold discipline from a child; if you strike him with a rod, he will not die. If you strike him with the rod, you will save his soul from Sheol. My son, if your heart is wise, my heart too will be glad (Prov. 23:13–15).

> The rod and reproof give wisdom, but a child left to himself brings shame to his mother (Prov. 29:15).

> Discipline your son, and he will give you rest; he will give delight to your heart (Prov. 29:17).

What Method of Discipline Is Appropriate?

In general, we seek to find appropriate cause and effect consequences. Suppose my child left his or her bicycle in the driveway when he or she had been told not to. That child would lose the privilege of riding the bike for a few days. Suppose my children were being goofy and careless when drying dishes (tossing them to a sibling across the room for instance) and broke one of them. Accidents happen, but if their foolishness unnecessarily caused destruction of property, I would require them to buy a new dish. Obviously, these decisions need to be made, ideally, by both father and mother, and the age and maturity level of the child needs to be taken into consideration. We encourage both parents to discuss discipline together and get on the same page to maintain a united front. It's never wise to allow your children to play one parent against the other, so finding unity in your marriage is key to your success in parenting.

Learning Repentance

Through discipline, children learn the steps of repentance, restitution, reconciliation, restoration, and redemption. If children never learn to have contrition when they are young, they will have a very difficult time doing it later in life. If they never learn to say, "I was wrong; I sinned," they will be more hardened to the idea as time goes on. They need to learn to humble themselves, grieve and mourn over their sin, and seek and find forgiveness.

After discipline, children need to be comforted and reassured that you love them and want only what is best for them. Be willing to pray together with your child and seek the Lord to work in his or her heart. The goal is to help the child surrender his or her heart and will to God.

> But he gives more grace. Therefore it says, "God opposes the proud but gives grace to the humble." Submit yourselves therefore to God. Resist the devil, and he will flee from you. Draw near to God, and he will draw near to you. Cleanse your hands, you sinners, and purify your hearts, you double-minded. Be wretched and mourn and weep. Let your laughter be turned to mourning and your joy to gloom. Humble yourselves before the Lord, and he will exalt you (James 4:6–10).

Don't Merely Discipline: Encourage and Inspire

It is not enough to merely discipline your children; you also need to give lavish verbal affirmation reminding them of your love. It's not enough to correct; you need to give positive encouragement as well.

I would refer you to a chapter I wrote on "The Power of Affirmation" in our book *Pitchin' A Fit! Overcoming Angry & Stressed-Out Parenting.*

Adopted/Special-needs Children

I am not an expert on either adoption or special-needs issues. I am aware, however, that there is usually a substantive difference between a biological child who bonds with his or her mother for nine months in the womb, nurses at her breast, and shares her DNA, and a child who has been adopted out of a situation with fetal alcohol, drug influence in the womb, separation anxiety, reactive attachment disorder, and more. While adoption is a beautiful redemptive act, it is often more difficult than people expect.

Discipline that works for a biological child will not always work for children who have defined differences in nature or nurture. Also, children who have cognitive delays, sensory disorders, mental disabilities, or other special needs will need to be disciplined differently. It is so important to get discipline right — safe, effective, and constructive. In many of these cases, you should consult with specialists who are familiar with these issues. I believe discipline and proper enforcement of boundaries can still be implemented, but you can't expect what worked for most of your children to work for those who have deeper struggles.

The Role of the Church

It only takes a few unbalanced parents mistreating their children to bring a huge blight on the body of Christ. Pastors and church leaders need to be proactive in systematically teaching their congregations how to biblically discipline and train children. Every "churchgoer" should have heard, from the pulpit or in a special class, how to correctly administer child discipline. Parents should know that mistreating their child physically, emotionally, psychologically, etc., is a sin and a crime that there is no excuse for.

Knowing how much our Lord loves and values children, we must commit ourselves to raising children in a completely loving and biblical manner. We must never abuse the sacred trust our children place in us. We must learn to abandon anger, discipline consistently and only in love, learn biblical principles for child training, and eventually instruct others so they can do the same.

The Church must be an educational resource where families can learn what God's Word teaches about how to live together in normal relationship with each other.

Jesus truly loves the little children . . . all the children of the world. Little ones to Him belong. They are precious in His sight.

Chapter 12

Gospel-Centered Parenting

A mistake I made early on in my parenting was to simply use correction as a means to modify behavior. I would often tell my child, "You just hit your brother. You need to stop doing that. Be nice." On the surface, this sounds very reasonable. The problem is that it fundamentally misses the big picture. Let me illustrate.

When I was about 19, my mother did something unexpected. She bought a puppy — a German shepherd. We hadn't owned a dog in years, and it seemed really random. After the fact, she told me, "German shepherds grow to be very large dogs. I really can't keep a dog that big unless it is trained and knows not to jump on people."

I agreed this was true and debated mentioning that this should have been considered *before* the purchase of the dog! Quickly, the realization of why this was relevant to me personally crashed in on me. "So, I have signed the dog up for obedience classes. They start this weekend and run every Saturday for the next six weeks. I need you to take the dog for me and train her."

I didn't buy a dog because I didn't want a dog. Taking my next six Saturdays to train a dog I didn't want was not on my agenda, but what do you do? When it is your mother, you go.

The first thing I learned is that dog training requires a lot of tedium. You teach the same methods over and over. To paper train a dog, you need to get up in the middle of the night, even when it's cold and rainy. You need to continue the process of correction and reward . . . over and over. Consistency is the main thing. If you aren't consistent, you are wasting your time and money. The dog will simply not obey you. It's a contest of the wills — you versus the dog. Who will win? Basically, if you outlast the dog, you will be in charge, and the dog will obey you. You can tell a dog to sit and stay, put a steak in front of that dog, and that dog will likely starve before it will eat that steak without your command. That's how good the results are from consistent training. Older and wiser now, I sometimes wonder if my mother set this up for her dog or for me. I learned far more from this process than the dog did. It trained me how to train.

When I became a parent, I objectively recognized that many of the techniques I had learned in dog training also worked with children. Tone of voice, reward and consequence, and consistent follow-through were all effective in getting my children to do what I wanted them to do. If getting your child to do what you want (in the short-run) is the only goal, one can see why some parents utilize this wrongheaded style of parenting.

Parenting Hearts

The problem with this approach is that it fails to recognize that our children are not dogs. They are eternal souls. While B.F. Skinner and Ivan Pavlov would be proud of such behavioristic child-training techniques, we must be careful that we do not resort to a pragmatic approach to parenting. Pragmatism is the view that "whatever works is right" or "the ends justify the means" or "it doesn't matter how you get there as long as you get there." This is not biblical parenting. Some parents say, "I tried disciplining my children, but it didn't *work*." Define what you mean by the term "work." What is usually meant is that the child stops doing the bad thing and starts doing the good thing.

Point Your Children to Christ

The thing your child ultimately needs is not "good behavior" but the Savior! Ravi Zacharias once tweeted that "Jesus did not come to make bad people good. He came to make dead people live."

It is not our desire to merely promote "morals" and "being nice." When our children sin, we have a wonderful opportunity to present the gospel and show them how much they need to be saved from themselves. Today, I am far more likely to use an opportunity for discipline this way:

> Son, you just hit your brother. Why did you do that? What is going on inside of you that caused you to behave that way? Can you see that in responding that way it reveals how you care more about pleasing yourself than you care about pleasing your brother and blessing him? Can you see how you are putting yourself and your desires above him? What does this show you about what you are like? You are selfish. The reason you are so self-loving is because you got it from me. That's what I'm like as well. And so were all of our ancestors back to Adam. The Bible tells us, "Therefore, just as sin came into the world through one man, and death through sin, and so death spread to all men because all sinned" [Rom. 5:12].
>
> The reason we act the way we do is because we were all born with a sinful inclination inside of us to go our own way. "All we like sheep have gone astray; we have turned — every one — to his own way; and the LORD has laid on him the iniquity of us all" [Isa. 53:6]. We are not born morally good. We are born loving ourselves, rebelling against God and His righteous law, and sinning against our neighbors. "None is righteous, no, not one; no one understands; no one seeks for God. All have turned aside; together they have become worthless; no one does good, not even one" [Rom. 3:10–12].
>
> You see, son, none of us can just choose to be good. The Bible teaches that our natural inclinations are to fight against God's rule over us. "For I know that nothing good dwells in me, that is, in my flesh. For I have the desire to do what is right, but not the ability to carry it out" [Rom. 7:18]. We need God's Spirit living in us to teach us how to tell ourselves no and do what God wants rather than what we desire.

Granted, I do not run through this sermonette with every single infraction of the rules. But I have done exactly this with many of my children.

What We Can Do

In covenant relationship with God in the parenting process, there are things we can do and things we cannot. The thing I cannot do for my children is change their hearts. I cannot make my children love God, love others, and want to do the right things for the right reasons. That is outside of my control, and yet, this is their greatest need. This is the role of the Holy Spirit.

Here are some things I can and should do:

1. I can teach my children the truth (Eph. 6:4).

2. I can try to model how they should live by my own example (1 Cor. 11:1).

3. I can seek to protect them from harmful influences (Prov. 13:24; 1 Cor. 15:33).

4. I can try to create an environment that is conducive to spiritual growth (Ps. 1:1–3).

5. I can pray like it means something to me (1 Thess. 5:17).

Moralism vs. Holiness

We can train our children to look and act good on the outside. Only God can transform them within so their desires align with His. If we are not intentional, we may inadvertently send a message to our children that what we care about is them merely having "good manners." If our child has never been born again, what chance do they have of living a godly life? If they have never truly been regenerated by the Holy Spirit, how can they live up to the "Christian character chart" we bought and put up on the refrigerator?

I remember, years ago, talking with one of my friends who was raised in a conservative Christian homeschooling family. He said, "I've tried to be good and do everything right, and it just hasn't *worked for me.*" Soon after, he came out as a homosexual and is currently legally married to a man. I believe he did try to be good, but I don't believe he ever had a transformative encounter with the living God that fundamentally changed who he was on the inside. He was trying to live the Christian life as a heathen. That will never work.

I'm learning that when my children sin and disobey, they need to see Jesus. I will tell them, "You know this sin that you committed against your brother? That is why Jesus had to die — to save sinners like you and me." I always put myself in that place of needing the Savior as well. My children inherited their sinful flesh from me. We turn to Jesus, and we ask Jesus to save us from ourselves. Our children's greatest need is not better behavior, it is Jesus. If Jesus is living and working on the inside of our children, He can do what we cannot. Let's work and intercede toward that end instead of focusing on merely external performance.

Chapter 13

Will a Trained Child Depart?

> Train up a child in the way he should go (on his own
> customized path), and when he is old/older/grown, he
> will not depart/will return (Prov. 22:6, my paraphrase).

This passage has given parents and Bible teachers fits for many years. There are lots of different explanations regarding what this text is teaching (including a few various translations I've seen of the verse above).

If we do our job correctly as parents, does that mean that our children will never go down the wrong trail? What then of the dozens of families we know who trained their children well (imperfectly but in the right direction), and their children rebelled?

Does it mean that if we train our children correctly, they may still rebel for a time, but then they will always come back to our faith later after they have gotten the rebellion out of their system? What about the families we know where the rebellious child never does return to the faith?

So, which is it? Will they never depart, or will they return? I believe the answer to both questions is: Yes and no.

Here's what I mean: I believe the Proverbs are speaking about general truths, not making absolute truth claims. I don't believe there is any way we can assume that the Proverbs are absolute statements that are true for all people, in all places, at all times. For example (please consider):

> Do not be wise in your own eyes; Fear the LORD and depart from evil. It will be health to your flesh, and strength to your bones (Prov. 3:7–8; NKJV).

Are all godly people you know healthy? Or what about this:

> A slack hand causes poverty, but the hand of the diligent makes rich (Prov. 10:4).

> The generous soul will be made rich (Prov. 11:25a; NKJV).

Are all the diligent, hard-working (or generous) people you know rich? (I didn't think so.)

> No grave trouble will overtake the righteous, But the wicked shall be filled with evil (Prov. 12:21; NKJV).

Do you know any righteous who have ever had grave trouble?

> The hand of the diligent will rule, But the lazy man will be put to forced labor (Prov. 12:24; NKJV).

Unless he goes on welfare . . . then he may not need to work.

> Do you see a man who excels in his work? He will stand before kings (Prov. 22:29a; NKJV).

Have all the skilled craftsmen you know met with world leaders?

> The eye that mocks a father and scorns to obey a mother will be picked out by the ravens of the valley and eaten by the vultures (Prov. 30:17).

How many rebellious teens do you know who have had their eyeballs eaten out by birds?!

This is an issue of biblical hermeneutics. That is the study of how we understand each book or section of the Bible in context and through the lenses of its own literary genre.

So, am I saying the Proverbs are false? Absolutely not! Am I saying they aren't the Word of God? No way! They ARE true! However, they are true in the way that they intend to be understood

— as broad general statements of truth that generally apply to the world (but of which there will be notable exceptions — as I pointed out in the passages above).

The original Hebrew wording for Proverbs 22:6 states: "Train a child (according to his way). . . ." What does that mean? While I believe the Bible translators are correct in translating it "In the way he should go," that isn't what the text actually says. It's most likely what it means, but it's potentially broader than that. Some have used this to justify a child-centered approach to parenting, implying that if we train a child "according to his own bent," he will grow up going the right way. The problem with that view is that children don't know what is best for them. Their flesh will usually desire the wrong choice.

What I think it demonstrates is that whichever way you "bend the twig," your child will be likely to continue in that trajectory (for good or bad). If children are permitted to be willful and rebellious, you will have a hard time bending them back to the correct path. If they are led in a godly direction, they are walking in that road and will be unlikely to turn aside.

I hope that this shift in your perspective on the nature of the Book of Proverbs, and the hermeneutic method (or set of lenses) through which we should read it, will help you to make more sense of the entire book, including this difficult and troubling passage that has plagued so many guilt-ridden parents for so long.

Chapter 14

Why Some Children Leave the Faith

For Demas, in love with this present world, has deserted me (2 Tim. 4:10a).

Over the years, I have observed hundreds of Christian families who seemingly did all the right things in raising their children, yet one or more still walked away from the faith of their parents once they were old enough to make their own decisions. No parent wants to go through all the trouble of training his or her children in the way they should go, only to find them turning around to head in the opposite direction.

It seems that the response to this on the part of the parents is to either blame themselves entirely or claim they did absolutely nothing wrong as a parent. I remember one father saying to me, "My wife and I did everything right, and our four children still want nothing to do with us."

Really? You did nothing wrong as a parent?! Ever?! But to give the man the benefit of the doubt, I hope what he meant to say was that he did the best he knew. That would probably be a fair and accurate statement, not just for him, but for most of us as parents.

Some people rather glibly say in response to prodigal children, "God is the best parent in the universe, and His children went astray!" That is certainly true, but I'm not sure that gives comfort to the hearts of grieving parents or helps them to understand what they might have done differently to prevent such an outcome.

We all make choices — good and bad — that alter the course of our lives. Knowing that adult children make decisions over which we have little to no control may leave us feeling hopeless and helpless in this parenting process. How do we know our labor will not all be in vain?

I cannot make promises to you or present you with formulas that offer sure-fire outcomes of success. There is not always a one-to-one correlation between the actions of a parent and the actions or reactions of his or her adult children. I've talked to many young adults who wandered away, and then cycled back to the faith in their mid-thirties. Many of them have told me their decisions had nothing to do with their parents. They admit they didn't have bad parents; they just wanted to sin. So, I do not believe that sin and rebellion on the part of the child is always caused by bad parenting. It would be a terrible fallacy to assume that.

However, I do want to share some harmful mistakes that I believe often contribute greatly to the breakdown in relationships and in a child's desire to follow God. As a parent myself, I humbly appeal to you to consider these stumbling blocks.

They Refused to Say "Yes" to God

As we begin traveling on the path of the righteous, God progressively asks us to submit every area of our lives to His Lordship. For many families, they recognize God's call for them to be fully engaged parents. They begin to die to themselves and submit their will to His. Soon they begin to experience the freedom that comes from surrender and are happy they made the choice. Then God asks them to give up something else or asks them to join Him in a certain work. Sometimes, the cost of that sacrifice is more than the parents are willing to pay. In such cases, it almost always leads to their children rebelling against God and parents.

> A disciple is not above his teacher, but everyone when
> he is fully trained will be like his teacher (Luke 6:40).

Children follow the example of their parents, and if we want our children to be obedient to God in all things, we must teach them by our lives.

Parenting for Christians

They Allowed Their Children to Have Fools as Companions

Do you remember when we discussed the two most powerful factors in influence? Young people crave acceptance and usually find it in a peer group or clique (or gang). If a child is allowed to spend large segments of time around bad influences, he or she travels the path of disobedience and rebellion. I don't believe I have ever seen an exception to this rule. "He who walks with wise men will be wise, But the companion of fools will be destroyed" (Prov. 13:20; NKJV).

> Do not be deceived: "Bad company ruins good morals" (1 Cor. 15:33).

It is not wise to allow your children to spend large segments of time, unsupervised, with other young people. "Foolishness is bound up in the heart of a child" (Prov. 22:15a; NKJV). When you put three children who all have foolishness bound up in their hearts together, they make a very strong bond and often will engage in destructive behavior they would never consider alone.

> And though a man might prevail against one who is alone, two will withstand him — a threefold cord is not quickly broken (Eccles. 4:12).

It is very hard for young people to resist negative peer pressure. You should know who your child's friends are and, ideally, spend time with your children and their friends (rather than sending them away from you for "socialization").

They Refused to Discipline Their Children

Even after their children have run away from home and are living on the streets, I've heard parents say, "I loved my children too much to discipline them." Often, because of bad experiences they had as children with abuse or improper discipline, they choose to ignore God's Word and believe a lie that it is loving to avoid disciplining their children. Refusing to discipline a child is one of the surest ways to incline his or her trajectory toward hell. "You shall strike him with the rod and rescue his soul from Sheol" (Prov. 23:14; NASB). *This verse is not prescribing physically abusing a child.* The goal of discipline is never to harm a child, but to teach him or her to learn how to eventually govern him or herself under God.

They Disciplined Their Children Inconsistently or in Anger

Many parents were not raised in godly homes themselves where loving, consistent, predictable discipline was implemented. Far too many parents struggle with understanding the right way to apply correction to their children. When discipline is done in anger, in excess, or simply to vent the parent's wrath on the child, it leads to a heart of rebellion in the child.

They Refused to Demonstrate Love, or They Belittled and Verbally Berated Their Children

Very few parents understand the awesome power of their words. "I tell you, on the day of judgment people will give account for every careless word they speak, for by your words you will be justified, and by your words you will be condemned" (Matt. 12:36–37). Part of the dominion mandate God gave to Adam in Genesis was to name the animals. Adam even named his wife. In the Old Testament, parents seemed to have an almost prophetic ability to predict or determine the child's behavior and lifestyle by the name he or she was given. Examples are Abram, Jacob, Jabez, etc. Children tended to become what they were named.

I believe this is still the case today. I don't mean that if you are named "Bill" or "Suzy" you will become what your birth name means. However, as parents, we "name" our children every day. We tell them who they are. "You are such a pain! Why are you so lazy? Why can't you do anything right? I'm sick and tired of dealing with you!"

These comments are lodged deep into the heart of a child and shape who they become. A refusal to speak and demonstrate love and affection leads to a distant, cold, and often resentful relationship. That is why it is so vital to speak words of truth and healing into your child's life. "See that you do not despise one of these little ones. For I tell you that in heaven their angels always see the face of my Father who is in heaven" (Matt. 18:10).

I constantly tell our children things such as, "You are a blessing! We love you. Jesus loves you. You are special to us. I am very pleased with you." It is wonderful to watch them become the true things my wife and I speak into their lives.

They Love the World

Some people claim to be Christians yet are enamored by the world and things of the world. They are fed by a secular pop culture — a steady diet of worldly movies, worldly music, worldly games and activities, worldly reading material, worldly heroes and idols, etc. Children who are engrossed in the things of the world will not love God. You can't love the Creator and the commercial pop culture at the same time.

> Do not love the world or the things in the world. If anyone loves the world, the love of the Father is not in him. For all that is in the world — the desires of the flesh and the desires of the eyes and pride of life — is not from the Father but is from the world. And the world is passing away along with its desires, but whoever does the will of God abides forever (1 John 2:15–17).

Anti-Christian Education

There is no way you can underestimate the power of 10,000–15,000 hours of anti-Christian indoctrination that students receive in godless government schools from K–12. My education-focused books go into extensive research and theology on why Christian children need an explicitly Christian education. I strongly encourage you to read my other titles on this topic.

They Gave Their Children Freedom Too Early

There comes a time when parents need to let their children stand on their own two feet. However, this is not at the ripe old age of 14. Often when teens are allowed to work outside the home, spend a lot of time away from home, or make too many important decisions before they are truly prepared, it instills in them an independent spirit that wants to be away from the family all the time. They begin to think of themselves as adults or as equal with their parents, and they reject parental authority. Obviously, we are all working toward this goal, but don't let go too early! The exact age will vary for each family since every child is different. Determining when your child is ready to be launched requires a lot of prayer, wisdom, and counsel from godly influences in your life. When our children become adults, we can still have influence and give godly counsel (especially when they seek it out), but our dynamic changes from authority to mentor.

They Were Hypocrites — Holding Up a Standard They Refused to Live By

Some parents care only about their image and reputation. They lack proper character, so they try to compensate for that by having a good veneer of religiosity. Children see this as it truly is — phony and self-serving. They reject the faith that their parents supposedly embrace because they see that the life of Christ isn't real in the private lives of Mom and Dad. If you are a hypocrite, sadly the best you can hope for is for your children to emulate your hypocrisy. More likely, though, they will be more honest than you and will be blatantly and openly rebellious. "But be doers of the word, and not hearers only, deceiving yourselves" (James 1:22).

They Were Legalistic (Strictly Adhering to Laws That Aren't Biblical Laws)

We must obey every word that proceeds from God's mouth. We must do everything He commands. However, some parents have created a litany of legalistic rules, guidelines, and principles that are not biblically based. We want our children to understand what God is like and to walk in the Spirit, emulating God's nature and character. But we must be careful that we don't cross a line into judging others or thinking of ourselves highly because we follow a bunch of self-made rules.

For example, a man once told me that his little boy blurted out in a restaurant, "Daddy, those people over there don't love Jesus!" When asked how he could be so sure, he confidently replied, "They are eating white bread, not whole wheat." Admittedly, wheat is healthier than white when it comes to bread, but children can grow up confused about what is essential to the faith and what isn't. Parents need to clearly outline to their children the choices they make that are based on personal preference and which ones are based on scriptural commands. We all have what I call "house rules." We have to make decisions about what foods we will allow our children to eat, what media they can access, what clothing styles they can wear, etc. In our home, for example, we don't allow our children to drink caffeine. We explain to our children that this decision has nothing to do with God's commands; we just think it is best for their overall health (and our overall sanity!). We explain to them that it doesn't make them better or worse Christians because they don't drink caffeine. We teach them not to look down on other families that allow their children to do so. It's a preference. But we teach them that bearing false witness against their neighbor is wrong for all people, in all places, at all times. That is God's command. If children recognize the difference, you can still have conservative standards without being legalistic or creating little Pharisees.

> Woe to you, scribes and Pharisees, hypocrites! For you tithe mint and dill and cumin, and have neglected the weightier matters of the law: justice and mercy and faithfulness. These you ought to have done, without neglecting the others. You blind guides, straining out a gnat and swallowing a camel! (Matt. 23:23–24).

They Had Other Priorities Above Their Family

"For where your treasure is, there your heart will be also" (Matt. 6:21). Children know what their parents value. When we spend our time and energy pursuing our career, our golf game, our friends, or our own comfort and pleasure to the exclusion of our children, they are pained by the rejection. Even if we are home every day, our hearts can be far from our children. We can be busy chatting with friends online, reading a book, or simply caught up in our own plans or routine. "But if anyone does not provide for his relatives, and especially for members of his household, he has denied the faith and is worse than an unbeliever" (1 Tim. 5:8). Yes, we need to provide for the physical needs of our family, but it is even more important that we provide for their spiritual needs.

They Never Repented of Dishonoring Their Own Parents

I have often seen a man or woman rebel against his or her parents when he or she was young. Unless that person repents and seeks to reconcile with his or her parents, his or her own children often rebel and repeat the cycle. The best way to deter this process is for a parent to grieve over the sins of his or her youth and intercede in prayer on behalf of his or her own children so they will not replicate the same sins. Obviously, there are many cases where parents have died and reconciliation cannot be made, but in those cases, the parents can still express their remorse to their own children and let them know how shameful it was that they did not honor, respect, and obey their parents when they were growing up. "The eye that mocks a father and scorns to obey a mother will be picked out by the ravens of the valley and eaten by the vultures" (Prov. 30:17).

They Neglected to Model a Godly Marriage

I've seen dozens of situations where a family looked picture perfect until the children went off to college (or thereabouts). Then the parents split up. Upstanding church families often have constant fighting and upheaval behind closed doors. I'm not talking about an occasional argument or disagreement. That is part of any household. But constant tension and stress between a husband and a wife takes a definitive toll on the emotional stability of a child or youth. In such homes, the youth often reject the faith and many times struggle in their single years with relationships of their own.

One of the greatest gifts you can give to your children is to work on your marriage. Most children would rather their parents be okay with each other than with them. They know that if Mom and Dad can work things out, that provides stability for their future. But if Mom and Dad are constantly on the brink of divorce (even if only in the child's mind), the lack of peace and harmony disrupts their sense of well-being. When parents model disunity, anger, bitterness, and frustration, children often look at such a scenario and think, "I'm not sure why this Christian faith is supposed to be so great. I have friends whose parents don't profess to believe anything, and they like each other and get along." Our witness for Christ in our own home is the most powerful sermon they will ever hear.

And this second thing you do. You cover the LORD's altar with tears, with weeping and groaning because he no longer regards the offering or accepts it with favor from your hand. But you say, "Why does he not?" Because the LORD was witness between you and the wife of your youth, to whom you have been faithless, though she is your companion and your wife by covenant. Did he not make them one, with a portion of the Spirit in their union? And what was the one God seeking? Godly offspring. So guard yourselves in your spirit, and let none of you be faithless to the wife of your youth. "For the man who does not love his wife but divorces her, says the LORD, the God of Israel, covers his garment with violence, says the LORD of hosts. So guard yourselves in your spirit, and do not be faithless" (Mal. 2:13–16).

They Failed to Equip Their Children with a Biblical Worldview

Children don't acquire a fear of the Lord or a proper understanding of life by osmosis. "Come, O children, listen to me; I will teach you the fear of the LORD" (Ps. 34:11). Do you know that you can teach your children the fear of the Lord? You do this by the example of your life. Parents must emphasize godly character and teach their children to put on the mind of Christ. We must learn to think as He does. If a child has a secular philosophy of life, he will eventually live out the beliefs he holds in his heart.

Sometimes it is hard to know what your children really believe, especially if they are complacent, compliant types. They may not be outwardly rebelling or rejecting your instructions, but inside they may be quietly denouncing everything you believe in. You need a catalyst or a tool to pry the sealed lid off of the container of beliefs your child is keeping bottled up. You can and should institute systematic teaching and training, but you need to get feedback. Keep open, relational dialogues going with your children.

Look for opportunities to draw out your children. Do they express the same opinions and beliefs when talking with their friends as they do in discussions with you? Are they consistent in their views, or do they merely say what they think you want to hear?

You want to really get to know the heart of your child? Study the art of asking good questions. I learned a lot about the importance of questions as a means of teaching when I was studying the material for my books *Questions God Asks* and *Questions Jesus Asks*.

If you discover unexpected rebellion in your child, by all means take it seriously. Thank God that He was kind enough to let you see it so that you can pray and begin to deal with the problem. My book *Education: Does God Have an Opinion?* is a great resource for knowing how to apply a biblical worldview to all areas of life.

Higher Education

I mentioned earlier that 70% of all students who go to secular colleges or universities bail on their faith by the end of their freshman year. What many Christian parents don't consider is that not all so-called Christian colleges promote a biblical worldview. I can't tell you how many stories I hear from Christian parents who invested years of their lives in their children only to watch it get dismantled by humanistic professors in private Christian colleges. Before you send your child to college, make sure you read Ken Ham's essential book *Already Compromised*. It exposes the humanism that has deeply infiltrated even Christian colleges and universities.

Is It Too Late?

For the parent with a wayward child who has left home and has wandered from the faith, you may wonder, "Is there any hope at this point? What can be done to change his or her heart?" At this point in my life, we have not experienced a prodigal child scenario (our oldest is only 19 at the time of this writing). I am reluctant to write on issues that I have not personally experienced.

I do know that God has it in His heart to forgive wayward sons and daughters when they come to themselves and return in repentance. I know that we must pray that God will do what it takes to break their stubborn will. Praying that prayer may result in incredible pain and suffering for them in this life, but in eternity, it could be the difference between heaven and hell.

There are many other writers who have produced materials on dealing with rebellion in children. I would recommend investing in these teaching resources and carefully considering anything the Lord would speak to your heart related to this matter. We don't have unconditional guarantees of success as parents. We can't assume that our children will automatically choose the right path. But we should not be fatalistic either and assume that the enemy is stronger than our Savior. We have great and precious promises in God's Word, and we should cling to them with everything we have in us. By the grace of God, we will be united with all our children in God's Heavenly Kingdom.

I have no greater joy than to hear that my children are walking in the truth (3 John 4).

Chapter 15

The Perfect Family Syndrome

Whoever conceals his transgressions will not prosper, but he who confesses and forsakes them will obtain mercy (Prov. 28:13).

I had a unique childhood in many ways. My mother got saved when I was 12 and had a radical, life-changing, born-again experience. The next year, she started a national magazine for homeschooling parents that became the nation's longest-running Christian homeschooling publication. Like it or not, as a young teenager, I was thrown into a level of public scrutiny that I didn't expect and didn't always know how to handle. Because my mother was a baby Christian living with an unbelieving and abusive husband (my stepfather), our home situation was far from perfect. But since my mother wrote about her pursuit of biblical ideals and published stories from other families who were also seeking to walk a godly path, many people assumed that our family had it all together.

Living in a fishbowl isn't as fun as you might suppose. Sure, you get a lot of attention, but sometimes, it isn't the kind you were hoping for. You often wish that when you fail, no one would see or care. This is true for children of high-profile Christian leaders, pastors, missionaries, etc., but it relates to all of us in some way or another.

How do you deal with the pressure of maintaining a "perfect family" image all the time, especially in the social media age? How do you make sure the inside of the cup matches its exterior? How do you judge when you are making it and when you're falling short? What do you do when your family doesn't qualify for the cover of the next *"Perfect Christian Family"* magazine?

At some time or another, all of us have considered what it must be like to be really famous. I mean, famous to the point where you can't leave your home without being recognized by the masses. It may seem glamorous to some, but the weight of such a lifestyle would soon become crushing. Face it — most of us can't deal with the unwanted attention we receive now! All of us struggle from time to time with keeping a proper perspective amid curious onlookers.

My wedding to Brook was pretty high profile. Our wedding story appeared the next week in the *Arizona Republic* and later in the *Wall Street Journal* and many other national and international publications. Within weeks of being married, my wife and I were speaking at conferences, telling the story of how God put us together in marriage. We didn't ask for the media attention; it was just the path the Lord had chosen for us.

The pressure didn't lessen once we became parents. I remember once when we had four children under the age of seven. I was speaking at a conference, and we were eating lunch in a large cafeteria area with perhaps a hundred or more other people. My toddler had just finished eating and was starting to walk around our table. At a certain point, he got bored and decided to head out for more adventurous territory. He took about two steps, and I called to him to come back to me. He turned around, looked at me, thought for a moment, and then took off running in the opposite direction. I bolted out of my seat, caught up with him, turned him around, and knelt down so I could look him in the eyes. Just as I was about to speak to him, I heard a woman's voice over my shoulder saying to her friend, "This is great! Now we can see how a REAL EXPERT handles a situation like this!"

For better or for worse, we are noticed. We are scrutinized and examined from every angle. Not to be presumptuous, but I would wager (just an expression, please don't write) that your family is under inspection as well. Maybe it's on a smaller scale, but it exists just the same. How do you deal with it? We want to strive to reach the standard of perfection God has commanded, but we know we all fall short in many ways. We want to be mindful of our witness to others, but we mustn't live our lives based on the expectations of other people.

What Is the Standard?

The biggest struggle in this area is to maintain a proper perspective. We must keep in mind what perfection is, how we discover it, and what to do if we fall short. "As for God, His way is perfect. . . . God is my strength and power, and He makes my way perfect" (2 Sam. 22:31–33; NKJV). Not only is God Himself the standard of perfection, but He is the only source of strength from which we can attain perfection. We constantly keep the face of God before us. We look not to the right or the left, but fully ". . . on Jesus, the author and perfecter of faith . . ." (Heb. 12:2; NASB).

How do people generally respond to the standard of perfection? In my experience, there are a couple of reactions.

Despising Any Standard of Holiness

I've noticed that people tend to reject any absolute that makes a demand on their lives. The call of Jesus requires that we surrender everything. As Dietrich Bonhoeffer stated in his foundational book, *The Cost of Discipleship*, "When Christ calls a man, He bids him to come and die."[1] We have received no other call than to give up our own lives for the sake of the call.

We often rebel against such a yoke. Autonomous humans want to be their own god. They want to make their own rules. They don't want any external imposition. Allow me to give a few examples.

When I attend Christian conferences, I listen to as many of the other speakers as I can. Sometimes, my workshop schedules prohibit this, but I like to check out the ideas of others. One session I attended featured a woman speaker addressing other parents. After a few minutes, she made the statement, "I'd like us to look at the 'Proverbs 31 woman.' " The lady in front of me leaned over to her friend and said, "I hate that 'Proverbs 31 woman'!" I laughed out loud at such an impromptu statement, but her remark was quite telling.

I've heard dozens of people comment on how they hate blog posts and book covers graced by "perfect" families: every child

---

1. Dietrich Bonhoeffer, *The Cost of Discipleship* (New York, NY: Collier Books, Macmillan Publishing Company, First Edition published in 1949), p. 99.

smiling, every hair in place, and everyone in matching outfits (which, by the way, are all clean!). One lady told me, "Those images don't reflect where I live. I have rowdy children and peanut butter on the walls." Even if those pictures don't reflect our personal experience, why do we rebel against them and despise them? Is it because we believe the featured family is being hypocritical? Or is it because we fear they may be genuine?

When we do seminars, people often approach us with questions about their children. Mothers tell us how their children are failing, then they turn to us and say, "But you wouldn't know anything about this. Your children are perfect!" The people who make these statements don't know us. They wouldn't know if we were "perfect" or not. They just assume that, since we are on the platform telling people about reaching for a godly standard, we must be superhuman. We get really nasty looks from some attendees who say, "So, are you always this nice to each other?" There is an obvious disgust, not only of our family, but of anyone who tries to call families up to a higher standard.

From their comments, it seems it isn't phoniness they dislike as much as it is legitimacy. If they could prove we were hypocrites, perhaps they suppose they can excuse their own imperfections. It appears they'd be happier to find out that we'd just had a big fight on the way to the seminar than to learn that our public image matches our private life.

Granted, our family is not perfect, just as your family is not perfect. We have our fair share of shortcomings, failures, sins, and character flaws. Like many others, sometimes we succeed, sometimes we fall short. However, we really do try to live out the life of Christ every day in our home.

Idolizing "Perfect" People

Then there is the opposite extreme. There are groupies who hang on every word spoken by a Christian leader. I'm convinced if some leaders told people to hang from a tree like a monkey, there are folks who would do it. The tough thing with these folks is that they look to another family as the standard and ignore God. When the groupie discovers an imperfection or sin in their idol, the faith of the groupie is shattered. They can't function. They can't pray. All they can think is, "If expert So-and-So couldn't make it, how can I?"

"I'll Never Be Perfect, So Why Try?"

I have found this attitude to be prevalent among many popular Christian authors. The whole concept of laughing off moral failure is completely unscriptural. We can't have a "stick a geranium in your hat and be sinful" mentality. I heard a popular female author on television say, "People are always saying, 'You need to hear from God.' I don't know where they get this stuff. I haven't heard from God in two years, and it hasn't stopped me! I just put my shoes on every day the same way I always have." (If she has read her Bible in the last two years . . . she's heard from God!)

This kind of flippant abandonment of holiness and godly standards of living is eating away at Christian homes. Without treading on too much theological ground here, it is faulty logic to say we should abandon our pursuit of holiness as unattainable ("nobody's perfect"). Hundreds of thousands of people play golf, knowing they will never hit a hole-in-one on each attempt. So why try? Why not purposely hit the ball in the woods? Why not land it in the pond or sand trap? In every field of life, we strive to be the best we can be. We mustn't fall short in our highest calling. We mustn't sin to enable "grace" to abound. That is nothing more than cheap grace, not the costly grace that our Savior bled and died for.

> Not that I have already obtained it or have already become perfect, but I press on so that I may lay hold of that for which also I was laid hold of by Christ Jesus. Brethren, I do not regard myself as having laid hold of it yet; but one thing I do: forgetting what lies behind and reaching forward to what lies ahead, I press on toward the goal for the prize of the upward call of God in Christ Jesus. Let us therefore, as many as are perfect, have this attitude; and if in anything you have a different attitude, God will reveal that also to you; however, let us keep living by that same standard to which we have attained (Phil. 3:12–16; NASB).

How Should We Respond to the Standard?

As believers, we have an obligation to be faithful to that which we know. The more we discover about the personality and character of God, the more obedient we must be. Scripture tells us we must actively live out our faith. Our actions prove what we really believe.

Why Must We Strive for Perfection?

First, because God demands it. "You therefore must be perfect, as your heavenly Father is perfect" (Matt. 5:48). (See also Gen. 17:1; Deut. 18:13; 2 Cor. 13:11; 2 Tim. 3:17; James 1:4.)

Secondly, we have an obligation to walk uprightly, setting an example for believers (1 Tim. 4:12). People need encouragement from others who are also striving for these heavenly goals. Like it or not, we represent Christ. That was the calling we received. We have a holy obligation to be faithful with whatever platform God has given us. "Be imitators of me, as I am of Christ" (1 Cor. 11:1).

We must never be like modern sports "heroes" who say, "I'm not going to be everyone's mother! I'm no role model." You are an ambassador for Jesus Christ, whether that is a good or bad image. We must run to and embrace the chance to be an example for others. We mustn't shrink back or hide in fear.

When We Don't Measure Up

Recognizing our need to be "salt and light," we can find that it's tough to deal with the reality that we're shining about as bright as a candle in the wind and tasting rather bland. However, we can't abandon our post. Deserters will have no part of God's Kingdom (Rev. 21:8). It's important to remember that (hopefully) we are all growing. Most of us have matured a lot in the last five or ten years. We should see things more clearly and do things better than we used to.

That is the work of the Holy Spirit in our lives, conforming us to the image of Jesus. We are in a discipleship process. Being an intentional parent gives you the context where you can see your child's needs. Spending lots of time with your child is the pressure cooker that boils carnality to the surface where it is visible and can be dealt with. Expect it. Plan on experiencing failures. The good news is, you don't have to stay there. We don't embrace a message of defeat but rather one of victory that says, "Sure, you're a mess right now, but you're growing."

We can't let our failures and foibles spoil what God wants to do through us. We need to keep short accounts with God. Keep the slate clean. If we do sin, "We have an advocate with the Father, Jesus Christ the righteous" (1 John 2:1b). Confess your sin, repent, and move on. There is too much work to do, and we should not allow our inadequacies or mistakes to keep us ineffective.

Just as we weren't born adults, knowing all things, we must grow spiritually as well as physically. I believe strongly in making spiritual landmarks as they did in the Old Testament. One of the purposes of these landmarks, besides marking private property, was to supply a long-lasting reminder of something important. It seems whenever God did something remarkable among His people, they built an altar or made a monument. They didn't want to forget. We should do the same thing in our families. No, we shouldn't pile up hundreds of rocks in our backyard! (We don't want the neighbors to start worrying about us!) We should, however, make spiritual landmarks whenever God gives us a significant victory in our home. Write it down in a journal. Get up in a meeting or family gathering and testify of some specific instance of God's goodness to your family. Make sure we don't forget. "But the path of the righteous is like the light of dawn, which shines brighter and brighter until full day" (Prov. 4:18). It's a process — don't give up!

How Should We Relate to Other Imperfect People?

The tough thing about getting the victory over a major hang-up is that we may lose compassion for those struggling with the very thing we just escaped. We found the answer and think they should receive the same revelation we did. Maybe they will, but it may take us some time. It took us a while. We agonized over it for months, maybe years.

We need to learn to give people space when they aren't like us. If they need to know something additional, God will show it to them. As Philippians 3:15 says, "Let those of us who are mature think this way, and if in anything you think otherwise, God will reveal that also to you."

We can't be the Holy Spirit for everyone else. We can lead them to living water, but we can't force them to drink. We can share what Christ has done in our lives, but they may not be ready for the change yet. That's okay. As long as they are still actively seeking God, they will find Him (Jer. 29:13).

If we need to confront a brother or a sister regarding a short-coming in his or her life, we should only do it if we are motivated by love. Don't shoot the wounded. They are probably already feeling guilty about missing the mark, and they need *encouragement* to make the hurdle, not rejection or judgment. We are to speak the truth (as hard as that can be sometimes), but we should do it only in love. We need to see the sinfulness of their hearts in light of the sinfulness of our own hearts. Only the grace of God enables us to walk uprightly. Without grace, none of us could live right.

Allow Inspection

Let's take advantage of the evangelistic opportunities the Lord sends our way. Because we have ten children, we stand out in many ways to others. People take notice of us and the way we live. We want them to see that what makes our family close, and why we really do love each other, is because of Jesus Christ and how He has changed our lives.

Don't hide behind closed doors, hoping no one will see the real you. If there are character flaws in your family, they need to be dealt with. Relationships can be like old food we leave in the back of our refrigerator that no one wants to deal with. The longer we let things fester, the smellier they will become! Be willing to hear the good and the bad from your mentors or those in your church or support group. That is what accountability and discipleship is all about.

Of what benefit is a support network where everyone is acting or pretending? Why not be real? Share your heart. If you're not doing well, don't lie. If your children are not in a good place spiritually, don't hide the truth. Ask for prayer and be willing to change if need be. If you have a rebellious teenager, don't cover it up and make excuses. Face it honestly. Only then can you be a true help to him or her. If someone confronts you about the behavior of one of your children, thank them for caring enough to let you know. Stop living with the guilt of skeletons in the closet. Clean it out! Get rid of it and start over.

A Brother Loves at All Times

We need covenant brothers and sisters who are willing to walk with us on this road of discipleship. I'm not sure where our family would be without godly people who are willing to love us unconditionally. Sometimes that love motivates them to gently rebuke us for short-comings. Other times it moves them to embrace us in our tears or to pray for us when we face seasons of doubt.

If you have people like this in your life, thank God and never take them for granted. If you don't have these faithful friends, try being that for someone else. God does not desire for your life to be 100% output without supplying friends to encourage and uplift you.

Remember, the key is to walk together in integrity. "And we all, with unveiled face, beholding the glory of the Lord, are being transformed into the same image from one degree of glory to another. For this comes from the Lord who is the Spirit" (2 Cor. 3:18). Throw away the masks! Allow the transformation to take place. Carnality is like a cancerous growth — the longer you ignore it, the faster it kills you.

Allow yourself to be accessible even to the members of your own household. After all, the goal is family-based discipleship. If your husband, wife, parent, sibling, or child sees a character flaw in your life, repent and change.

Set an Example for the Believers

The Apostle Paul told the Church at least three times to be imitators of himself (see 1 Cor. 4:16, 11:1; Phil. 3:17). We see this pattern also in 1 Thessalonians 1:6, 1 Timothy 4:12, and Hebrews 6:12, as well as Hebrews 11. It is not wrong for others to look to our behavior as a guideline for holy living. Are we not to be imitators of Christ? Therefore, in our conduct, speech, and all other aspects of our lives, we must seek to uphold God's standard of holiness in absolute purity. We have received no other calling. This is truly the call we heard from Christ: to give all we are for all He is. Let us embrace it and rest in it.

Our world needs love. It is also in need of leaders who aren't afraid to stand up and be counted. We can truly represent Christ in this post-Christian culture. As the Body, we need each other more now than we have at any other point in American history. The world needs us. Christ is calling. Will we answer?

Chapter 16

Helping the Difficult Child

My wife and I have often commented that we are thankful that not all our children were easy to raise. We've had some that are relatively complacent and compliant. My wife says that some of our children were born with their shirts tucked in and their hair combed! All children have a strong will that exhibits itself in different ways and times, but some are much easier than others to lead and guide. Having children who are strong-minded and challenged has helped us to empathize more than we would otherwise be able to when working with families whose children struggle.

As a child, I was dyslexic and hyperactive with attention deficit disorder. We have children who have been clinically labeled with certain diagnosed issues, but all children have strengths and weaknesses. We are not experts in any way when it comes to dealing with special needs or clinically difficult children, but we hope that some of our thoughts will be useful for you.

God Gave This Child to You

The Almighty makes no mistakes. Your child wasn't sent to you by accident. God knew that you were the parent your child needed and that he or she was the child you needed. This parenting process is just as much about our sanctification and spiritual growth and maturity as it is about our child's. We need to be willing to embrace the painful process of raising this difficult child, knowing that it will do a vital work in our own hearts.

Don't Make Excuses for Your Child

It's important that parents don't make excuses for bad behavior. If my parents had said, "Israel has a chemical imbalance, so we can't expect him to obey," I would have been a literal terror. We need to be willing to listen if other people bring their concerns about something naughty our child just did. We shouldn't defend our child's actions when he or she is truly out of line, but we also need to be realistic about our expectations regarding our child. Especially children with special needs cannot always "perform" in the way they may be expected to by others, or even by us. We need to be aware of their limitations and not expect them to transcend where they are not capable.

My mother always knew the difference between being active and being unruly. There is never an excuse for dishonor or disobedience. Should children be disciplined every time they get excited? If so, we wouldn't have accomplished much else when I was growing up! There must be a certain amount of tolerance given to children or else they will become bitter, but children should always know what behavior is appropriate and what isn't.

Most of our years growing up, my mother was the only parent (at least the only functioning one), so all discipline fell to her. She allowed us to have fun, but when she indicated that things needed to calm down, we knew that meant immediately. She wasn't the type of parent who would tell the child three times before expecting a response. If we disobeyed, we were disciplined. That's how it worked. After a while, we began to see a pattern. When Mom speaks and we ignore her, we get disciplined. When we obey, we don't get disciplined. Soon, people were asking my mother, "How do you get your children to obey you on the first request?" The trick was she convinced us that she wasn't speaking just to hear her lips flap.

I don't want you to get the feeling that my mother was overbearing or severely strict. She wasn't. In fact, other mothers complained that they disciplined their children twice as much as my mother but didn't have the same results. Because Mom was so consistent, she rarely had to discipline us. She just spoke . . . once.

Active Is Not the Same as Disobedient

Again, keep in mind that there is a definite difference between rebellion and being lively. Rebellion, if not dealt with, will explode and become uncontrollable in the teen years. Children who have never been expected to obey will not suddenly become polite, responsive individuals at adolescence. By refusing to immediately deal with rebellion, parents teach their children to disobey and dishonor them. If rebellion is dealt with at an early age, parents won't need to worry as much about major problems in the teen years.

In my case, I wasn't usually purposefully obnoxious or unruly; I was just full of energy and had a hard time restraining myself when a thought popped into my head. When I thought something, I did it (or said it). When I was three, for example, our Sunday school teacher asked my class, "What do you want to be when you grow up?"

Each child took his or her turn with standard answers like, "I want to be a farmer, or an astronaut, or the President." When my turn came, I innocently stated, "I want to be fat and ugly, like Mr. Ross [our church deacon]." Laughter filled the classroom as the teacher tried to control the pandemonium. (I know I didn't have very lofty aspirations, but I answered truthfully. As a somewhat undersized youngster, from my point of view, Mr. Ross was the pinnacle of human perfection.)

Many children probably would have been severely reprimanded for such a remark, but my mom knew that I really liked Mr. Ross and meant no harm in what I said. Instead of disciplining me, she merely worked on helping me improve my social graces.

Training Is for the Child's Good

Knowing how to respond to difficult behavior is the real key. Learning the balance between knowing when to discipline, when to instruct, and when to just lighten up and laugh is the challenge facing parents. When I did something outrageous or embarrassing, my mother would have to evaluate my motives. Was I being disobedient, disrespectful, inconsiderate, selfish, etc., or were my intentions pure?

Sometimes, parents care more about their own image than they do about the development of the child. My mother never disciplined me simply because I had embarrassed her (which I did constantly), but she was always concerned for my spiritual well-being.

A good illustration of this would be an evening meal we had when I was four. My parents were concerned with making a good impression on our dinner guests. The family finally arrived for dinner and we all sat around the table to eat. The visiting family wasn't used to praying before the meal, but they politely allowed us to thank the Lord for our food. While we were praying, the man and his wife were looking at each other rather nervously. I could tell they weren't Christians because they didn't keep their eyes closed while we were praying. (Don't ask me HOW I knew they didn't have their eyes closed!)

After the prayer, there was an awkward moment of silence, as no one really knew what to say next. I was frustrated by the fact that no one was talking. So, never at a loss for words, I proceeded to get to the heart of the problem. "Mister, you're goin' to hell — and so is your wife and so is your kids!" My mom choked and stuffed a biscuit in my mouth, and Dad remembered something he had left on the burner. Their whole family turned a dark shade of purple, and we finished the rest of the meal in virtual silence.

When they left that evening, I nearly cried, realizing the perilous destiny of this family and our complete failure to adequately communicate it to them. Now, some parents would have waited until their guests were safely in the car and out of earshot, and then proceeded to threaten the devil out of their child. My mom, however, knew my intentions, and although I had completely embarrassed her, she didn't discipline me. (In the overall scheme of things, she didn't discipline me for a lot of the things I did because they weren't acts of rebellion or disobedience; they simply indicated that I needed to learn appropriate restraint.) Instead, she sat me down and explained a better means of handling the situation. If I ever did repeat a mistake that we had discussed, it showed that I had crossed the line from ignorance to disobedience or apathy. Disobedience and apathy were not acceptable.

Distinguishing just how to discern where pure motivation clashes with deliberate disobedience in the difficult child comes down many times to knowing your child. For youngsters that don't readily pick up on relational cues or have a sense of empathy, it may require much more in the preparation department. This takes investing strategic time with them in non-crisis moments. It is important with our difficult children to draw them close and keep them close to us. In spending that extra time with them, we can gain clues to how our children perceive the world around them and how we can prepare them for various scenarios that emerge in their relationships.

Many times, the difficult child can feel such a sense of frustration when it seems he or she receives a lot of correction. This is where it is crucial that we as parents be in tune with our children to really know the motivation behind their behavior, never allowing sinful demonstrations to rule, but kindly leading our children in what is right. And this is also where we need to carefully examine our own motives. Our interactions with every one of our children, difficult or not, need to be for their benefit, never out of our embarrassment, to serve our convenience, or to make ourselves look good, but truly out of love. Christ-like love will always bear fruit, and that's a good promise (see John 15).

Chapter 17

Serious Fun

Every parent has weak spots. Interestingly, one of my major deficiencies as a father is the opposite of most other men.

One of the things I try to avoid are those father/son retreats, where dads and their sons bond together in the rugged wilderness. It's not that I don't enjoy connecting with my sons — far from it — it's just that I have a hard time relating to that context.

Most other fathers seem to have figured out how to create fun memories with their children (especially their boys). They take them hunting, fishing, camping, kayaking, etc. They teach their children how to build tree forts, fix the car, rebuild an old bicycle — lots of essential life skills. They also take their children on annual family vacations to water parks, amusement parks, theme parks, zoos, museums, sporting events, etc. Most dads know how to be the hero who leads their children in grand and memorable adventures.

None of this comes naturally to me at all. As I've gotten older, I've started to understand why. A lot of it goes back to my childhood. My parents divorced when I was 6, and I saw my father for one weekend a month until I was 15, and then he wasn't a part of my life for 23 years. We lived with my abusive stepfather from the time I was 6 to 15, but all I ever learned from him was how to be an angry person. He never gave me any positive life skills.

I graduated from homeschooling a few days before my 16th birthday and immediately started working full-time outside the home to help financially support my single-parent mother and five sisters. In many ways, I had to grow up the hard way. My mother, God bless her, had to not only be the mother, but she was also the provider. I've never known anyone who worked harder than my mother. She sacrificed immensely for her children, living on four hours or less of sleep a night for years and working 18 to 20 hours a day (in between homeschooling and being a mother). I couldn't even begin to match her tenacity or willpower. Somehow, she started a successful publishing business from scratch, fed and clothed six children, homeschooled them, never took government assistance (from the time she became a Christian when I was 12), and managed to keep us out of debt.

We pulled together as a family to make the best out of a terrible situation, and God blessed it. Because of the tremendous financial strain of just trying to survive, we didn't grow up with a lot of free time or luxuries. Family vacations were something we seldom had time to do. A couple of times my mother did find a way to arrange them (which I'm sure was at great sacrifice), but for the most part, we learned to enjoy our work and to have fun in doing something productive (rather than taking time off to do nothing but relax).

A Strong Work Ethic

There is no doubt we are shaped by our childhood. I know I am. In terms of personality, I'm wired a lot like my mother. I'm fairly driven in terms of wanting to work hard and achieve goals. I have high expectations for myself and those around me. I'd rather be accomplishing something important than sitting around wasting time.

I have noticed that a lot of other men work hard and then shut it off and relax with their families. This is extremely difficult for me to do. My mind seems to almost constantly be in work mode. I'm often distracted instead of being in the moment with my family because I'm feeling the tug of projects that need to be completed or deadlines that are looming. Having my own business only complicates this tendency.

Suppose my family wanted to go to the beach and visit one of the many lighthouses that dot our beautiful Lake Michigan coastline where we live. As I'm walking with my family, looking at the seagulls and watching my children run up the sand dunes, the whole time I'm thinking about how I can't afford the time and how much I'm not getting done in the office.

Changing Course

The reason I'm sharing all of this is because if we can't recognize our weaknesses and be brave enough to change course, we can create devastating consequences in our relationships. Every child responds differently to his or her circumstances. My response to my childhood scenario was to embrace it and make the most of it. But not all my children are wired like me. I need to be sensitive to that.

It is very possible to be around our children and yet not be giving them what they truly need from us.

One thing that I think I do well, that perhaps 90% of other fathers struggle with, is discipling my children in God's Word and truth. While I was not raised with daily family devotions, I made a commitment early on in our marriage that this would be a regular part of our life. I've been pretty consistent with our spiritual disciplines, by God's grace. I'm strong on proper teaching, instruction, and consistent discipline. At the time of this writing, I have a good relationship with every one of my (now) ten children, but I am learning that I need to adjust my sails.

Another father, who also speaks at conferences as I do, was telling me about the road trip he took with his family traveling from event to event. He said they stopped to see Mount Rushmore, Laura Ingalls Wilder's childhood home, the museums in Chicago, etc., etc. He asked me what my family did. "Well, we pretty much drove for 15 hours, unpacked, set up for a conference last Thursday through Saturday in Virginia, then I spoke at two different churches on Sunday in Pennsylvania, then I did a seminar on Monday night in Ohio, then another on Tuesday in Indiana, then drove another 12 hours on Wednesday, and set up on Thursday for another event. . . ."

I could tell he wasn't impressed. "So, what do you do for fun?" he asked. "What are your hobbies?"

"Fun?" I had to think. "Hobbies? I guess for fun, I work. And I spend time with my family. We read books together, or we . . ." (I was going to say I play board games with them, but I really don't. I'm too busy and can't focus because I'm thinking of all the important things I'm not doing when I try to play a game.)

Here's the deal. I don't really have a need to take time off to "have fun" because I enjoy my work. I don't usually need a break from it to feel good. But my children are NOT wired that way. They need uninterrupted time that is designated to nothing but just having fun for the sake of having fun.

As my oldest became teenagers, I tried hard to intentionally change my habits. It hasn't been easy, but I'm making some improvement.

One Sunday, my wife wasn't feeling well, so she stayed home on Sunday morning while I took my (then eight) children to our church meeting. After the service, I took the children to the park. Not just any park — THE park. The park with all the really amazing features. Then we went to a ball field and played baseball. Then we went swimming in the pool. After that, we watched a movie and ate dessert.

That night, my seven-year-old daughter said, "This has been the best day I ever remember! Ever!"

Her words were both rewarding and painful at the same time. She was simply getting what many children get on a regular basis — Dad's undivided attention.

A Need for Balance

As I said, we are all off-kilter in some respect as parents. Maybe for you it's hard to be disciplined and get academics done with your children. Maybe you are too lenient in terms of discipline. Maybe you want to be a buddy to your child so badly, you aren't being a strong enough parent. Perhaps you know how to have fun, but you can't seem to get the needed spiritual training to happen consistently. Whatever it is, I want to encourage you to be honest with yourself and be willing to accept feedback from your family, or those outside your family, who may see your blind spots better than you do. In my case, I don't think any of my children are angry or resentful for the shortcomings I've expressed here. I think I'm more aware of my deficiencies in this area than they are, but if I don't make the necessary improvements in how I relate to them, I know that my imbalance will lead to needless relational problems down the road.

We are all in process as parents. There is no shame in recognizing that we sin and fall short in our role as family leaders. The good news is that we don't need to stay stuck. We can change by the grace of God and often through the help of God's people.

In my case, I need to learn how to lighten up and just enjoy having fun for no good reason. For you, it may be something entirely different. But whatever your weakness, don't wait until it is too late relationally before you allow the Holy Spirit to make the necessary changes in and through you.

Remember, God opposes the stubborn and proud, but He gives much grace to those who are humble and acknowledge their need for Christ.

Chapter 18

Hospitality: It's Not Just for Women Anymore

For a bishop must be . . . a lover of hospitality (Titus 1:7–8; KJV).

They say a man's home is his castle. I'm not sure what that means, but there have been times when I've thought it would be nice to have a moat around my house. I don't mean to sound antisocial, it's just that after a long day of hard work, or a weary road trip, I'm ready for a nice quiet evening with my wife and children.

There is nothing quite like a recliner, a lap full of children, and a good storybook to help me unwind. You must admit, life is stressful. For some of us, the thought of adding one more thing to the mix just doesn't appeal. So, what happens when your wife (or husband) is particularly given to hospitality, and you are not? In my case, it's not that I don't like people; it's just that I prefer that they enjoy their own homes and let me enjoy mine. I mean, after all, good fences make good neighbors, right?

When Brook and I were first married, we had the ideal home. A small, quaint, country setting that you couldn't find even if you knew where to look. To get there, you had to take a county road to a dirt road, to another dirt road, and then suddenly pull onto a long driveway that wound back to our house, which was nestled near woods and a pond. My work at that time required me to interact with people over the phone, and sometimes in person, all day long! After hours of communicating I was ready for some peace and quiet.

My wife, on the other hand, desired from the beginning to be a stay-at-home wife and mother. After a nice quiet day at home (it became less quiet with each subsequent child!), she would sometimes say to me upon my return, "It sure would be nice to have some guests over for dinner." My assessment was that there are some people "given to hospitality" and some who are not. I assumed that I was in the latter category and my wife was in the former.

Given to Hospitality

One day I was reading 1 Timothy 3:2 regarding the qualifications for an elder or bishop, and I noticed that the requirement "given to hospitality" (KJV) was in the list. It appears also in Titus 1:8, only stating more strongly that we must be "a *lover* of hospitality" (KJV; emphasis mine). The Scripture is clear about the heart of God concerning this issue. God is not looking for reluctance but extravagance when it comes to giving of ourselves for other people. The Greek word used in both passages is *philoxenos*. It means literally, "a love of guests."

The word appears again in 1 Peter 4:9: "Show hospitality to one another without grumbling." That means the act of serving someone else, in itself, doesn't win you any brownie points. It must come as a genuine act from the heart. Romans 12:13 presents a unique idea by using the Greek word *dioko* for "given" to hospitality (KJV). The implication is that we are to pursue hospitality as though we are chasing something that we desire to overtake. That surely isn't passive!

It is through hospitality that you will develop lifelong friendships, provide the right kind of friends for your children, and perhaps even get to know the future spouses of your children.

Practical Considerations

Some children naturally take to social environments and automatically reach out to others to help them feel welcomed and at ease. Most children, in my experience, do not have those innate qualities. They need to learn the skill of hospitality through observing us leading the way.

Although we are no longer in the "boondocks," we travel extensively around the country. This can also cut down on our opportunities to interact with other local families on a regular basis. We have found that it is helpful to be a member of a Christian travel network that links people of like faith and allows them to share their homes with weary travelers. We have often enjoyed the fellowship of families who were traveling through our area, and we have stayed in the homes of people who hosted us when we were on the road. Many of these precious people have become dear friends. We have found this to be a wonderful experience all the way around.

1. It allows us to meet new people that we would never otherwise encounter.

2. It gives our children the chance to learn to serve others who visit, or conversely, how to be considerate guests.

3. It provides unique cultural experiences by learning about other parts of the country and the customs and beliefs of other Christians who don't live near us.

4. It saves us money when we travel because we aren't paying expensive motel costs.

5. It helps us to see more practically how God has His people literally all over this country, many of whom are learning the same things we are.

It lets us use our home as we believe God intends, as an expression of His heart of love for people. I would encourage you to reach out in love and take a risk to show hospitality to those around you or those across the nation whom you may not yet know. It will honor God and will bless you, for as the Scripture says, ". . . It is more blessed to give than to receive" (Acts 20:35).

Children will not usually embrace a desire to serve others unless they see it modeled in their parents. In all the areas we want our children to grow, we should be growing. That is how discipleship works. Our children see us succeeding in important areas of life, and it gives them a roadmap for success as well.

Chapter 19

Living on One Income (Brook)

But godliness with contentment is great gain (1 Tim. 6:6).

Investing my life in my family is one of the greatest privileges in my life. Not only do I believe my place in God's Kingdom is to serve as a mother during the season when my children are in my home, but I also love doing it. I believe one of the things that makes home discipleship possible for us is that we have made a way for me to stay at home with my children instead of working outside the home. Some people believe that this is a matter of privilege. They believe some people are born wealthy enough for such a luxury and some are not, but I can assure you that has not been the case in our family. We have had to fight hard to make it work, as have hundreds of other families we know. We weren't handed this option on a silver platter.

In a society obsessed with money and possessions, where two-income households are the norm, living on one income can be financially and culturally challenging, but it is not impossible.

Truly Desperate?

I do realize that there are desperate circumstances that require both parents to work. There are real needs for food and clothing that necessitate less than ideal situations. But, frankly, many families live as if the situation were more desperate than reality requires. These families are sending both parents into the workforce to get a paycheck to maintain an "above-the-basics" lifestyle. These choices result in a general inability to walk out Deuteronomy 6:7's instruction to teach God's Word diligently to your children when you rise up, when you lie down, when you sit in your house, and when you walk by the way. Not having your children with you hinders time to talk as you do life together. Does this happen simply to keep starvation away from the door and simple clothing on the family? Certainly, there are desperate situations, but I fear that what many of us are willing to call "desperate" is just a bad case of living for and clinging to material gain.

One such example is the true story of a young mom who thought their situation was "desperate," so she returned to the workplace to supplement her husband's adequate salary, putting her four-month-old and two-year-old daughters into childcare so that the family could fund a debt-laden mortgage payment of a half-million-dollar home in a wealthy neighborhood. Oftentimes, "desperate" is however we personally define it (see Matthew 6 for Jesus' definition). The Bible is very clear: What gain is it truly if we accumulate the wealth of the entire world and yet forfeit our very souls or, for that matter, our children's souls (see Matt. 16:26)?

I respect the story of the widow who lived around the turn of the twentieth century. Hers was a desperate situation, and with six little mouths to feed and six backs to clothe, she knew she had to come up with some sort of income. Not willing to leave her God-given post as a mother, she took in the laundry of more well-to-do folks, and from dawn until sundown she scrubbed, washed, wrung, hung to dry, and pressed clothing. She poured her physical strength into completing her job and, at the same time, poured her heart into instructing her children. The family ate corn and beans every day, every meal. But they were together, and the Lord watched over them.

What Price Will You Pay?

I wonder how many of us would eat corn and beans for a season if it came down to that? Would we embrace what this widow gave up in order to stay faithful in our posts as parents? Obviously, it is not responsible to be lazy or negligent in the care of our children; however, many parents are driven by an insatiable quest for MORE, rather than being content with basic necessities.

It is important to ask ourselves these kinds of questions: Would you give up your second vehicle? What about moving to a smaller home? Would you stop eating out at restaurants? Would you pass up buying designer clothing or even new clothing? What price are you truly willing to pay in order to boldly keep your little ones under your training?

If our own situations warranted it, would we be willing to cut way back on our grocery budget, electricity usage, or gift expenditures in order to properly raise our children in the fear of the Lord? Could we give up steak and ice cream? Our children need financial provision, but they need spiritual and emotional provision far more.

For many parents, a double income is sought not for extravagance but to try to dig out of a severe financial pit. How do you get out of the grave of debt? Well, it will probably necessitate professional budget counseling, accountability, and a map to financial freedom. It requires embracing a new lifestyle of saying "no" to frivolous spending, bad decisions that damage your credit, and living above your means, not to mention an enslaving mentality of defeat. View financial debt as your mortal enemy, because it is. It prohibits your ability to make the best choices for your family.

Cutting the Strings

We live in a culture that is more than willing to define for us what we "must" have. Advertisements shout that we need this or that, pumping lies into us that life is just not complete unless we have our culturally perceived "needs" (often more accurately labeled "wants") met. On top of this, your own circle of social interactions can be a huge influence on your perceptions. If everyone you know purchases a new vehicle every year, you are likely to pity yourself for driving a ten-year-old, used vehicle. If all your friends can afford to go out to eat once a week, the tendency is to feel sorry for yourself that going out to eat twice a year is a big deal.

Our happiness simply cannot rest on financial status. Paul had it right when he wrote, "Not that I am speaking of being in need, for I have learned in whatever situation I am to be content. I know how to be brought low, and I know how to abound. In any and every circumstance, I have learned the secret of facing plenty and hunger, abundance and need" (Phil. 4:11–12).

Contentment is such a big deal that the Scriptures call it great gain. In worldly terms, great gain means financial gain or material wealth. Certainly, material wealth is one of the avenues God chooses to bless His people, but sometimes He allows our circumstances to be such that He provides bounteous opportunities for greater gain. "But godliness with contentment is great gain" (1 Tim. 6:6). And verse eight makes it clear just what we ought to be content with: "But if we have food and clothing, with these we will be content."

If we stop listening to the culture around us and change our influences, chances are we'll start seeing things in a whole new light. Perhaps it will even go so far that we won't see the heap of "sacrifices" we've had to make in order to be effective parents, but we'll start seeing how graciously the Lord provided and how faithful He is to care for those who walk according to His ways. Change your influences by learning about the real needs of the persecuted Church and the desperate situations millions of little children face in other countries. Change your influences by choosing to have your emotional needs met by the Lord and not by a shopping spree.

Choose to celebrate life, anniversaries, birthdays, etc., with a focus on giving thanks and fellowship and not so much on receiving gifts. Paul said he has learned to be content with times of much and times of little. For the effective parenting team that lives on one income, remember the purpose is to accomplish a goal — to obey God by diligently training His children. There is no virtue in stinginess, but rather the opposite — God loves the cheerful giver! "Each one must give as he has decided in his heart, not reluctantly or under compulsion, for God loves a cheerful giver" (2 Cor. 9:7). Live freely, generously, and yes, abundantly, choosing to live apart from the culture's dictates.

Another practical idea is to begin keeping a journal of God's provision. Record the special instances that He provided and read back every so often to remind yourself of His care for you. When we start seeing how faithful He has been to provide, our hearts can really turn to gratefulness. As Matthew Henry said, "Children are God's gifts, a heritage, and a reward; and are to be accounted blessings, and not burdens: He, who sends mouths, will send meat, if we trust in Him" (*Matthew Henry Concise Bible Commentary* on Psalm 127:3).[1]

We've become very conditioned in our country to constantly compare ourselves with "the Joneses." There is nothing innately wrong with enjoying fine things or shopping. The problem comes when/if we let the pursuit of material/lifestyle gain sidetrack us for the calling God Himself has placed on our lives as parents. Second Peter 2:19b says we're slaves to whatever has the mastery over us. Fear of giving up comfort and luxury has kept many a would-be missionary at home. Clinging desperately to this world's stuff keeps many people outside the gates of heaven. I plead with you, don't let the love of this world and its possessions lure you away from faithful, effective parenting.

When we fully obey the Lord, there is no need to fear for tomorrow. "But seek first the kingdom of God and his righteousness, and all these things will be added to you" (Matt. 6:33). Fear for tomorrow is a choice, and in order to move forward with the Lord, we need to disentangle ourselves from its grip.

"No soldier gets entangled in civilian pursuits, since his aim is to please the one who enlisted him" (2 Tim. 2:4). Have you set out to win in the race of raising godly children? Then don't let the culture of the love of affluence entangle you.

> Therefore, since we are surrounded by so great a cloud of witnesses, let us also lay aside every weight, and sin which clings so closely, and let us run with endurance the race that is set before us (Heb. 12:1).

---

1. BibleHub.com.

Chapter 20

Allowance — What Should Parents Do?

Many parents rightfully desire for their children to learn good financial stewardship. To help children develop a budget and learn to manage their money responsibly, many parents give their children a weekly or monthly allowance.

What Is a Standard Allowance These Days?

What do other parents give their children? According to a 2019 survey by the American Institute of Certified Public Accountants (AICPA), 86% of Americans believe children should receive allowances, most starting by the time children reach age 8; 52% say it should be linked to chores. On average, children are spending about 5.1 hours a week doing chores to earn their allowance; 66% of parents give their children a regular allowance that is their money to keep.

Spanning all age groups, allowances average $120 per month, averaging $6.11 per hour for chores (according to the Bureau of Labor Statistics).[1]

Is an Allowance a Good Idea?

The Bible doesn't speak to this issue directly, so there isn't a moral absolute here, but let us share with you our perspective.

We have never given our children a regular, set allowance.

1. https://www.aicpa.org/press/pressreleases/2019/childrens-allowance-pay-is-up-amount-saved-alarmingly-low.html.

The primary reason for this is that we do not want our children to develop an entitlement mentality (which is WAY too common in our society today). Many people believe that they should be given money simply because they exist. The Bible always links the earning of money with labor. "In all toil there is profit, but mere talk tends only to poverty" (Prov. 14:23). We want our children to develop a strong work ethic and to become producers in society and not mere consumers, living off the labor of others.

Paying Allowance for Chores?

Because of these concerns, many parents have made the choice to link allowance to household chores. We do not do this either. Again, not a moral absolute, but we believe that being a part of the family means that everyone works together as a team to make the household work. We all (even the parents) have assigned tasks that we do for the love of the other members of the family.

We, as parents, do not get paid to wash our own laundry or make our own bed. This is not how finances work in the real world. We want our children to learn that if they want to get paid in real life, they must provide a product or a service that is of value to others. If they are not producing something others want, they aren't making money.

So, we do not pay our children for doing regular household chores. We encourage them to think entrepreneurially and to find real products and/or real services for which other people, outside of our family, are willing to pay. This may include raking a lawn for a neighbor or knitting baby blankets for sale, etc.

Paying Our Children for Special Projects

We are blessed to have our own family business, so this is a wonderful opportunity for us to pay our children for legitimate work they do. Anything they contribute to our business, whether it is packing and shipping orders, sorting receipts for tax purposes, handing out promotional literature at events, etc., is all legitimate work that in some way, directly or indirectly, produces a real income. They are paid for all such efforts.

We highly recommend that families strongly consider starting a family-run business that everyone does together, specifically for this purpose of teaching children good work habits, genuine career skills, and creating earning opportunities. It is rare that such businesses are ever able to earn enough to support the family entirely, and in most cases, a family-run business will never net as much as a paid salary from an established company, but whether or not the business becomes a primary means of financial support, it is invaluable in teaching skills, entrepreneurship, and financial stewardship in a real-life context.

One other thing for which we will pay our children are projects that we would likely hire out to an outside agency. If we would pay someone else to do a job for us, then we will pay our children. This will look different for every family, but for us, things like lawn maintenance, snow removal, small household repairs, and cleaning leaves from low hanging gutters in the fall (for the older teens), etc., are all opportunities for us to fund our children (again, usually teens) instead of paying someone outside of our family.

Work Ethic

If children don't learn to work when they are young, they will likely resent it when they are teens. We have found that one of the best ways to teach children to work is to have them work with us. Instead of sending them outside to rake leaves, they enjoy the work so much more if they get to be with us and serve alongside us. Children don't usually enjoy being "sent." They want to be led. They want us to lead them into adventures, and they catch most of what they see modeled in us. That is why balance is so important for us as parents. We are creating the template they will follow.

Teaching Financial Stewardship

Regardless of whether you agree with our allowance model, we hope that you will teach your children to budget, save, and give, realizing that the money we receive as Christians does not ultimately belong to us, but to God. We are His managers or stewards, and we need to spend His money only as He wants us to. Money is a great servant, but a terrible master.

Chapter 21

Passing the Baton — Teens/Young Adults

> Do you not know that in a race all the runners run, but only one receives the prize? So run that you may obtain it (1 Cor. 9:24).

Imagine a runner sprinting as quickly as he can in his section of a relay race. When he reaches his partner, who is to receive the handoff, he stretches out his arm with the baton extended, in every hope that the runner ahead will be able to receive the transfer successfully. The next runner begins running forward, not looking back, with his arm behind him, waiting to feel the baton in his hand. As soon as the transfer is made, the second runner begins sprinting with all his might in the direction of the goal. Once the second runner has the baton, the first runner's job is done. He has done everything he can and should do. It is now the second runner's turn to finish the race.

In many ways, this is a great analogy for what we as parents are hoping to accomplish with our children. We want our children to receive the baton of truth. We desire to pass on moral values, convictions, spiritual vitality, good study habits, self-control, godly character, honor, good relationship skills, etc.

There is so much that is represented by that baton. We run the parenting race for 18–20 years; then it is time to pass on that baton. If there is a time when the baton will be dropped in a relay race, it is almost ALWAYS at the crucial juncture of handoff. Once the baton is in the runner's hand, he rarely lets it go. But it is so common to see a team fail at handoff, and the results are always devastating.

Raise Adults, Not Children

The goal of parenting is to raise an adult, not a child. When my children reach the age of 20 (give or take a year or two), I hope that I will have successfully instilled in them everything they will need to be prepared for life. For better or worse, what I've taught them by that age is pretty much all I will be able to teach them (in a developmental sense).

If I have done everything in my ability to transfer my beliefs and values to my children, then I need to trust my own parenting. If I think my ideas about life are correct (that I have planted the best ideological seeds in their lives), then I need to trust that what I have planted will (eventually) grow to fruition. Even more important than trusting my own parenting, I need to trust the Holy Spirit to continue to work in these young adults' lives. I don't want to cushion them from every bad decision. I don't want to micro-manage their lives. I don't want to be the Holy Spirit for them. I want them to learn to fly using their own wings. I want to pray for them and be available to answer questions they ask, but I am expecting them to be adults, not dependent children. If I have raised them to be dependent children, then I have done myself (not to mention them) a grave disservice.

Don't Expect Them to Embrace All of Your Values

When my children are small, they must abide by my standards. I am their parent, and I am the boss. I tell them what to eat, what to wear, when to go to sleep, when to get up, and what to believe. I am doing my best to bend the twig in what I perceive to be the best direction. All good parents and educators do this (whether intentionally or not).

I have very conservative standards and rules for my home. My young children don't get a vote. However, I am well aware that when my children approach adulthood, they need to learn how to reason and discern on their own. I don't want them to adopt my values merely because they are my values. I want my children to do what they believe God requires of them in His Word. I would rather see one of my children reject one of my closely cherished personal standards because they felt the Bible teaches them otherwise than I would for them to blindly embrace my view without having a clear reason why.

In the end, my fellowship with my adult children is not rooted in our common standards (as much as I hope they may look similar). Our fellowship will hopefully be rooted in our common faith in our common Savior. As parents, we need to discern what hills we are willing to die on. For myself, I hope that my children will love God with all their heart, mind, soul, and strength, and love their neighbor as themselves (Matt. 22:37–40). If they do this, I will consider myself to be a successful parent. If they choose (for some weird reason) not to live in the country, raise chickens, and eat homemade whole-wheat bread, then I will not disown them (even though I will lament the fact that they are really missing out on the good life — just kidding!).

I don't expect my children to think and live exactly like me. I expect them to think and live like Jesus. I am going to faithfully, and without apology, teach and live out what I believe the Bible teaches. I fully expect my children to do the same, although their expression of their faith may look different than mine.

Maintaining Peace in the Home

Sometimes you reach an impasse with an older teen or adult child who has decided that he or she cannot abide with your standards. The young adult may have planted his or her feet and will not comply with your responsibility to govern your own household. Sometimes this can create tension, especially if you have younger children for whom you are still accountable. Perhaps the younger children are embracing the negative views of their older siblings and are prematurely attempting to exert their independence. In those situations, it may be necessary to have a parting of ways between that older child and the rest of your household. Hopefully this doesn't need to be a bloody battle. Ideally, this can be a mutual understanding that you are no longer able to live together in a mutually compatible arrangement. I don't believe that this parting needs to be viewed as either inevitable with every child at some arbitrary age or as a relational failure. It may simply be a necessary part of the baton-passing process.

The parent can affirm the adult child's right to make his or her own decisions (media choices for example), and the young adult should recognize his or her parents' desire (and right) not to have certain influences in their home. Hopefully, this can be worked out in a manner that is beneficial to all parties. The adult child may just need to find his or her own place to live. Again, I don't have easy solutions to all these issues. I trust God to give you grace and wisdom if you reach such an impasse. I also hope that you have respected Christian friends or church leaders who can help to provide godly wisdom and counsel for your family in these matters.

Passing the Baton

As I am running toward my child, trying to pass on my faith and values, I don't want to let go of the baton too soon. I want to ensure that my child is in motion, arm extended, ready to receive it. I want to be certain that he or she has firmly grasped the handoff before I let go.

However, when I do let go, I want to genuinely let go. I don't want to run around the track, hanging on to the baton so that my child won't drop it! I don't want to run alongside him or her, yelling instructions about how to run the race. Instead, I want to catch my breath and cheer him or her on. If my child starts to run off-track, I will send up a prayer and trust that all the training I've given him or her will pay off. I will trust that my child will quickly regain his or her view of the finish line and renew his or her stride. Advice and counsel to young adults needs to be given sparingly (if at all) because advice that isn't sought is usually not well received.

While I am currently my child's coach, I look forward to the day when I will be his or her biggest fan. I want to make the most of my opportunities, and I truly hope my children will run well when it is their turn. If they falter or stumble, I don't want to give up on them. I believe that God will be merciful to them, to teach them despite their imperfections and mistakes, just as He has been to me. I don't care if my child's running style is different than mine; what is important is that we are on the same team (assuming this is the case) and that we will someday both receive the prize for having run well.

My hope and prayer for all Christian parents is that they will be successful in transferring what really matters (a love for the Lord and others) and will be willing to let go of the things that aren't essential. May the Lord grant us grace to be gracious to one another and successfully pass on the baton, not merely from one generation to the next, but from generation to generation to the next generation, and so on, for the glory of God.

Chapter 22

Parenting by Grace

Therefore it is of faith, that it might be by grace. . .
(Rom. 4:16; KJV).

I was sitting on the platform of a Christian parenting conference, looking out over the audience. This was one of those end-of-the-day Q&A sessions where the exhausted main speakers field questions and try to think on their feet. One of the other speakers had the microphone and was waxing eloquent about the wonderful virtues of fathers being leaders in their homes.

His general synopsis was that dads should lead their wives and children or else we could expect to see an entire generation of young people go off the deep end spiritually and morally. He cited statistics of what happens to young people who are raised in homes where the dad is not actively involved in their lives. He explained the break-down of the American family and how divorce was wreaking havoc on young lives. He stated how children are much more likely to be involved in violent crime, experience unwed pregnancies, experi-ence domestic abuse in their marriages, get divorced themselves, and on and on, if the parents are divorced and/or the father is not positively involved in the family.

It was a rather surreal moment for me. Knowing that the micro-phone would soon be passed to me for my comment, my head was spinning. I found myself wanting to nod my head in approval and shake it in protest all at the same time. On the one hand, he was so right.

When I was a volunteer chaplain in the juvenile justice system, I asked about 300 young men about their relationships with their fathers. Most never knew their dads, or their fathers were completely absent from their lives. I only remember one or two cases where a young inmate said he had a good relationship with his father (and those were first-time minor incident offenders). There are dozens of studies on the direct impact of absent (or relationally absent) or harsh fathers, and the connection to juvenile delinquency. The facts seem clear to me that young men with proactive fathers just don't end up in juvenile crime. The leader on stage was so right.

Despite my general agreement, another part of me felt really conflicted. If this view was correct (that without a godly father in the home, children are doomed to languish in spiritual lethargy and/or moral decadence), how could I explain my situation?

As I mentioned previously, my parents divorced when I was 6. My mother, who was not a Christian at the time, remarried, and I lived with a very physically abusive stepfather for the next 9 years until he eventually found someone else and moved on with his life. We were not exactly the poster family for godly "family renewal"! I could identify experientially with everything the other speaker was saying. At 15 years of age, I too was becoming a statistic. I was becoming angry, violent, and bitter. Our family was a mess and getting worse all the time.

My mother did her best, but we just had such a deficit to recover from. *So*, I thought, *I guess the other speaker is right. Without a good dad in the home, you are just up the creek without a paddle.*

Something kept nagging at me, though. *He's forgetting something*, I thought to myself. Then it hit me. I could sum up in one word what was missing from his presentation: grace.

When I was 12, my mother met God. She wasn't out looking for Him. He just intervened in her life in an amazing and powerfully transformational way. Her "Damascus Road" experience was enough to get the attention of myself and my five sisters. I've never seen anyone get as sold out to Jesus as my mom did. When she met Jesus, we were living in poverty, fear, and defeat. We had been through welfare, battered women's shelters, and homelessness. We knew what it was like to be dysfunctional. We had no idea what it meant to be a godly family. Even churches didn't want us showing up for services because we made them look bad.

As I sat on that stage, so many years later, it was hard to believe that the life I experienced had such beginnings. The difference between my childhood and now is 180 degrees. The fact that God has seen fit, in His divine providence (and sense of humor), to give us a national ministry to families is beyond comprehension.

In God's great mercy and kindness, He allowed Brook and me to start our marriage off on the right foot. We had a clean slate and have had no regrets in our marriage. We have ten beautiful children (so far) who bless us every day. We are excited about teaching and training them in the ways of the Lord. We are blessed that we get to teach other people the biblical principles that we have learned about godly family relationships. I'm spoiled rotten.

I can trace all these blessings back to one decision, and it wasn't mine. My mother, looking at the prospect of raising six children all alone, with no husband and no financial security, decided to trust God with her whole heart. Proverbs 3:5–7 are verses she lived out consistently. My mother humbled herself and received God's grace (James 4:6). I have received residual blessings from the changes in her life.

God is truly the husband to the widow and the father to the fatherless (Ps. 68:5). God proved Himself to be sufficient for us in every way. My mother had nothing going for her except that she trusted God completely. She didn't even finish ninth grade! She had no job skills and no means for making a living. When she became a single parent, we didn't even own a car! We had no chance at all of making anything of our lives. There was only one word that stood between us and utter ruin: grace.

When God intervenes in a situation, He does the impossible. He uses the foolish things of this world to confound the wise. He uses the weak things of this world to confuse the strong. He can take a family that is messed up, full of bad choices and mistakes, and He can make something beautiful from all the mess. It necessitates absolute surrender. It takes throwing yourself on the mercy of God. It requires giving up and refusing to run your own life one day longer. It means letting Christ take control of every facet of your existence. He wants complete, total, and final Lordship of everything that you are.

Now don't get me wrong. I'm not down on men taking leadership in their homes. Because of what I've lived through, I think I am way more intentional about being a servant-leader in my home than I would have been otherwise! I'm intense about fathers leading their children in family worship and being godly role models. I'm all about Malachi 4:6 and seeing fathers turn their hearts to their children.

What I've learned, however, is that if God uses a man to lead his family in paths of righteousness and his children learn to walk in truth through his instruction and nurture, that is a work of grace. If God raises up a generation of men who are not going to wimp out like the generations before them (and I see this happening all over the country!), that is a work of grace. If the Christian community is carried into the next generation on the shoulders of godly men who love their families and lay down their lives for their wives and children, that is a work of grace.

The point is, it really isn't about us as fathers, at least not ultimately. It's all about grace.

It isn't about faithful single parents who lead their children as the lone sanctifying spouse. It isn't about Christian mothers trying to do their best while living with uninvolved, ambivalent, or non-Christian husbands. It's all about grace.

As much as I love my mother and thank God for her faithful example, it really isn't about her. It's all about grace!

Anything good that we have in life is an undeserved gift from God's hand. The way we avail ourselves of that grace is through humility. We must come to the end of our rope and admit that there is a God, and He is not us. When we are finally broken and surrendered to His will alone, He will raise us up. Whether you are a single mom or a faithful, Bible-teaching male leader of your home, it isn't ultimately about you. It's all about God and His marvelous grace. Throw yourself on the merits of Christ and watch in amazement what He can do in and through you and your family.

About the Authors

Israel Wayne and his wife Brook are homeschooling parents to ten children (five boys and five girls) ranging in age from nineteen years to nine months, with four teenagers still living at home. They have had a lot of opportunities to put into practice what is in this book.

Israel Wayne is also an author and conference speaker who has a passion for defending the Christian faith and promoting a biblical worldview. He is the author of:

Education: Does God Have an Opinion?
Pitchin' A Fit! Overcoming Stressed-Out Parenting
Questions God Asks
Questions Jesus Asks

Since 1995, Israel has traveled the nation speaking on family, homeschooling, revival, discipleship, and cultural issues. He is a frequent guest on national radio and television programs and has been featured as the keynote speaker at numerous conferences. Israel also serves as the Director of Family Renewal, LLC.

The only wisdom we have, we received from God. If the revealed Word of God is not your starting point, you will be very frustrated with our book, which relies on a lot of Scripture, because we believe God knows better than you or we do. — Israel Wayne

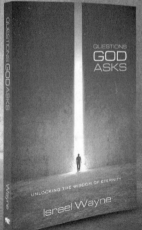

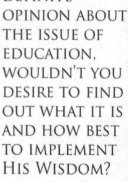